WITHDRAWN

NEW ESSAYS ON THE SUN ALSO RISES

GENERAL EDITOR

Emory Elliott, Princeton University

Other books in the series:
New Essays on The Scarlet Letter
New Essays on The Great Gatsby
New Essays on Adventures of Huckleberry Finn
New Essays on Moby-Dick
New Essays on Uncle Tom's Cabin
New Essays on The Red Badge of Courage
New Essays on Light in August
New Essays on The American

Forthcoming:
New Essays on Chopin's The Awakening (ed. Wendy Martin)
New Essays on Ellison's Invisible Man (ed. Robert O'Meally)

New Essays on
The Sun Also Rises

Edited by

Linda Wagner-Martin

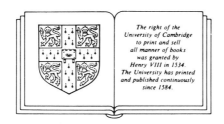

The right of the
University of Cambridge
to print and sell
all manner of books
was granted by
Henry VIII in 1534.
The University has printed
and published continuously
since 1584.

CAMBRIDGE UNIVERSITY PRESS

Cambridge

New York   New Rochelle   Melbourne   Sydney

Published by the Press Syndicate of the University of Cambridge
The Pitt Building, Trumpington Street, Cambridge CB2 1RP
32 East 57th Street, New York, NY 10022, USA
10 Stamford Road, Oakleigh, Melbourne 3166, Australia

© Cambridge University Press 1987

First published 1987

Printed in the United States of America

Library of Congress Cataloging-in-Publication Data
New essays on The sun also rises.
(The American novel)
Bibliography: p.
1. Hemingway, Ernest, 1899–1961. Sun also rises.
I. Wagner-Martin, Linda. II. Series.
PS3515.E37S924   1987   813'.52   86-33414
ISBN 0 521 30204 8 hard covers
ISBN 0 521 31787 8 paperback

British Library Cataloging-in-Publication data applied for.

Contents

v

Contents

5

Decoding the Hemingway Hero
in *The Sun Also Rises*
ARNOLD E. AND CATHY N. DAVIDSON
page 83

6

Afterthoughts on the Twenties
and *The Sun Also Rises*
JOHN W. ALDRIDGE
page 109

Series Editor's Preface

In literary criticism the last twenty-five years have been particularly fruitful. Since the rise of the New Criticism in the 1950s, which focused attention of critics and readers upon the text itself – apart from history, biography, and society – there has emerged a wide variety of critical methods which have brought to literary works a rich diversity of perspectives: social, historical, political, psychological, economic, ideological, and philosophical. While attention to the text itself, as taught by the New Critics, remains at the core of contemporary interpretation, the widely shared assumption that works of art generate many different kinds of interpretation has opened up possibilities for new readings and new meanings.

Before this critical revolution, many American novels had come to be taken for granted by earlier generations of readers as having an established set of recognized interpretations. There was a sense among many students that the canon was established and that the larger thematic and interpretative issues had been decided. The task of the new reader was to examine the ways in which elements such as structure, style, and imagery contributed to each novel's acknowledged purpose. But recent criticism has brought these old assumptions into question and has thereby generated a wide variety of original, and often quite surprising, interpretations of the classics, as well as of rediscovered novels such as Kate Chopin's *The Awakening*, which has only recently entered the canon of works that scholars and critics study and that teachers assign their students.

The aim of The American Novel Series is to provide students of American literature and culture with introductory critical guides to

American novels now widely read and studied. Each volume is devoted to a single novel and begins with an introduction by the volume editor, a distinguished authority on the text. The introduction presents details of the novel's composition, publication history, and contemporary reception, as well as a survey of the major critical trends and readings from first publication to the present. This overview is followed by four or five original essays, specifically commissioned from senior scholars of established reputation and from outstanding younger critics. Each essay presents a distinct point of view, and together they constitute a forum of interpretative methods and of the best contemporary ideas on each text.

It is our hope that these volumes will convey the vitality of current critical work in American literature, generate new insights and excitement for students of the American novel, and inspire new respect for and new perspectives upon these major literary texts.

Emory Elliott
Princeton University

Introduction

LINDA WAGNER-MARTIN

MOST writers' first novels do not turn out to be their most important work. In Ernest Hemingway's case, *The Sun Also Rises* has gradually come to have just that reputation. After an intense four-year writing apprenticeship (to Gertrude Stein, Sherwood Anderson, Ezra Pound, Ford Madox Ford, and others), Hemingway wrote his 1926 novel with a sense of surety, a knowledge of craft, and a belief that literature could create morality. He produced a document of the chaotic postwar 1920s and a testament to the writer's ability to create characters, mood, situation, and happenings that were as real as life.

Readers reacted to the novel explosively. "Here is a book which, like its characters, begins nowhere and ends in nothing"; "a most unpleasant book"; "raw satire"; "entirely out of focus." Whether critics saw Hemingway's style as the flaw or, more commonly, his characters and their rootless, sensual ways, they were ready to condemn his choices of both method and subject. As the reviewer of the *Chicago Daily Tribune* exclaimed, "*The Sun Also Rises* is the kind of book that makes this reviewer at least almost plain angry." *The Dial* reviewer called Hemingway's characters "vapid," as shallow "as the saucers in which they stack their daily emotion."[1] Even Hemingway's mother agreed that his characters were "utterly degraded people" and that the novel might better have never been written.[2] Edwin Muir, writing in *Nation & Athenaeum,* stated that the novel was skillfully written but lacked "artistic significance. We see the lives of a group of people laid bare, and we feel that it does not matter to us."[3]

But there were also the avid Hemingway readers, those trained to appreciate his subtle efforts, his omitted details, through experience with his earlier short stories (*Three Stories and Ten Poems,* 1923; *in our time,* 1924; and *In Our Time,* the longer version, 1925). Cleveland B. Chase praised *The Sun Also Rises* for "some of the finest dialogue yet written in this country," Hemingway's "truly Shakespearian absoluteness"; Herbert S. Gorman, his creation of people "who live with an almost painful reality"; and Burton Rascoe, his impeccable style: "Every sentence that he writes is fresh and alive. There is no one writing whose prose has more of the force and vibrancy of good, direct, natural, colloquial speech. His dialogue is so natural that it hardly seems as if it is written at all – one hears it."[4] Ford Madox Ford as well championed what he called Hemingway's "extremely delicate" prose. Edmund Wilson found his style as well as his subject matter "rather subtle and complicated," and Hugh Walpole referred to Hemingway as "the most interesting figure in American letters in the last ten years."[5] Some of this critical attention was based on the sense that Hemingway was just at the beginning of his artistic promise. N. L. Rothman described his effective use of understatement to mask an inexpressible anguish, claiming that "there is a good deal in the writing of Ernest Hemingway that is being overlooked," and H. L. Mencken warned the young writer that he had achieved his huge success through "technical virtuosity," but that style alone could not maintain such a reputation.[6]

The most excited comments focus primarily on *style.* Hemingway burst on the modernist scene well acquainted with the current passion for innovation (we think of Ezra Pound, wearing his flamboyant scarf embroidered with the phrase "Make It New"). The modernist method was understatement, a seemingly objective way of presenting the hard scene or image, allowing readers to find the meaning for themselves. "Hard-boiled" was not exactly the right phrase, but it came close. No "sentiment," no didacticism, no leading the reader: The modernist work would stand on its own words, would reflect unflinchingly its own world, and would smash through the facade of "polite literature" that had dominated the Victorian era and turn-of-the-century American literature.

Hemingway, born in 1899, had been practicing his art ever since high school, when he wrote shrewd and quasi-humorous pieces for the school paper. After graduation he chose not to go to college but began working instead on the Kansas City *Star*, where his notions about true sentences and clear writing had their birth. After less than a year, in May 1918, he volunteered for the American Red Cross ambulance corps in Italy. His World War I experience ended with his being severely wounded near Fossalta (over 250 shrapnel wounds in his legs and thighs). He returned home after hospitalization in Italy, and the following winter he convalesced in Petosky, Michigan, spending his time writing. Michigan was beloved territory to him: He had spent every summer since his first birthday at the family cottage on Walloon Lake, near Charlevoix, and his love of the lakes and forests was to be indelible.

Several years passed. Hemingway was working in Chicago, writing for himself (imitating Sherwood Anderson's *Winesburg, Ohio,* which had been published in 1919) and for *The Cooperative Commonwealth* (for a salary). After his marriage to Hadley Richardson in 1921, he went with his wife to Paris, partly to write for the Toronto *Star* but, more importantly, to live the life of the expatriate writer and to learn all he could about writing. His first published work was poetry. Then he wrote the tirelessly polished vignettes of *in our time,* which became the one-page interchapters of the 1925 *In Our Time.* Ezra Pound had praised these for their "clean hard paragraphs" and had gone on to link Hemingway with James Joyce and Ford Madox Ford.[7] The young writer's accomplishment, even before publishing a novel, was considerable.

Pressure on Hemingway grew; he wanted to become more widely known and to leave his apprenticeship status behind. During July 1925, when he and Hadley had returned from a second trip to Pamplona, Spain, for the bullfights and the running of the bulls, he began his first novel. The Hemingways, along with Duff Twysden, Pat Guthrie, Don Stewart, Harold Loeb, and Bill Smith, had tried to recapture the good feeling of their first visit to Pamplona in 1924, which they had made alone; but the relationships in the 1925 group were so divisive that the resulting tensions lasted for years. *The Sun Also Rises* is sometimes called a roman à clef because many of its characters are identifiable as real people: Brett Ashley is modeled on Duff (and was called Duff in the early drafts of the book); Robert Cohn on Loeb; Jake Barnes on Hemingway (and was called Hem); Romero on the bullfighter Cayetano Ordoñez. The work of fiction, however, far surpasses this somewhat limiting description of it as "gossip."

Determined to write a masterpiece, Hemingway set out to write a first novel that he himself called "moral." And *The Sun Also Rises* – despite all of its seemingly loose living – moves toward a highly moral, even noble, ending. In Brett's relinquishing of Pedro Romero, a man she sincerely could have loved, comes her moment of truth. Its chilly truthfulness is emphasized in her abrupt phrasing, almost shocking in its terseness: "I'm not going to be one of these bitches that ruins children" (243). Jake, too, comes to realize how improbable his love for Brett has been; and even when she makes overtures to him after Romero has gone, he treats her wryly and sidesteps any further involvement. The concluding scene of the novel is famous for its understatement:

> "Oh, Jake," Brett said, "we could have had such a damned good time together."
> Ahead was a mounted policeman in khaki directing traffic. He raised his baton. The car slowed suddenly pressing Brett against me.
> "Yes," I said. "Isn't it pretty to think so?" (p. 247)

For the first time in the novel, Jake's great love for the mysterious, forthright "new woman," Brett, begins to diminish. What that lessening finally indicates is left open, however. Will Jake and Brett remain friends? Will they ever again play at being lovers? Will the group re-form back in Paris? Will they ever return to Pamplona? Most important, how will the future lives of these characters develop? And will they ever escape the brutalizing effects of the war?

Like most of Hemingway's fiction, *The Sun Also Rises* steers clear of giving the reader the "meaning" of the book, neatly wrapped and summarized. The ideal modern novel was to involve the reader, to suggest myriad possible interpretations. The novel shares with many other great fictions this "open" ending, in which the reader is left to think about what the closing scene or scenes might indicate. Hemingway wants the reader to sense Jake's new realism even while he remains helplessly caught in his love for Brett. He is not suggesting that Jake's feeling for Brett has changed, that Jake

4

dislikes her, or that the powerful chemistry that has led Brett to wire Jake, asking him to rescue her from Madrid, has ended. What has ended is Jake's belief that he and Brett will work through their problems and come to live happily, simply, together.

The Sun Also Rises is more than just a romance. If the whole plot were dependent on Jake's getting or losing Brett, the novel would hardly have kept readers coming back to it for sixty years. In the complications of the Jake–Brett romance lies Hemingway's remarkable ability to catch the temper of the era. Starved for affection, victimized by her former husband, Brett is a product of war-ravaged Europe. She must have physical affection, in quantity, for reassurance. And just as Brett is maimed by her experiences of World War I, so is Jake. His wound, however, is a physical one. As he looks in the mirror of his apartment, he thinks, "Of all the ways to be wounded. I suppose it was funny" (30). Even though Jake manages to feel sexual desire, the act of intercourse is physically impossible. In his dramatic staging of Jake's conflict, Hemingway succeeds in giving the reader an image of war damage that is inescapable and poignant. Whenever Jake is on stage, which is most of the time, his wound permeates everyone's awareness. And since the ostensible action of the book usually involves Brett's amours, Jake's injury is omnipresent.

If the mood of postwar America was disillusion and frustration, then Jake's physical incapacity is a striking image of many kinds of disability. The loss of promise after World War I was one of the chief reasons for the expatriation of America's writers and artists. Failure of belief in all of the traditional panaceas (religion, politics, economics, romance) led to the bleak "waste land" atmosphere so evident in T. S. Eliot's poem of that name (1922) or Theodore Dreiser's 1925 novel *An American Tragedy*. The mood of American and British literature alike was tentative, more subdued in tone than it had been for fifty years. The brilliance of Hemingway's novel was that it appeared to fit into that mood while actually contradicting it.

Hemingway worked carefully to achieve this ambivalent effect. He began with an epigraph that he attributed to Gertrude Stein: "You are all a lost generation." (By the time of his writing *The Sun Also Rises*, he was less enthusiastic about Stein's writing, and her friendship, than he had been during the previous four years, so there may be some malice in his linking her with this line.) His notebooks record that the phrase was in reality spoken to Stein by a garage mechanic, using the French (''c'est un generation perdu''). According to the mechanic, the lost generation was that between the ages of twenty-two and thirty: ''No one wants them. They are no good. They were spoiled.'' There is no question that war has damaged the lives and psyches of Hemingway's characters, but Hemingway intends that there be some recognition of the value of that ''lost'' group who have survived the war, even if imperfectly.[8]

The quotation attributed to Stein comes first on the epigraph page and is immediately followed by the passage from Ecclesiastes from which the title is taken. *The Sun Also Rises* is as affirmative as the biblical passage and is in strange contrast to the idea of the lost generation. It is as if Hemingway were contradicting Stein, her friends, and the pervasive tenor of their comments about those people affected by the war. Characteristic of the way poets use fragments of conversation, scenes, and images in a poem, Hemingway is building the structure of the novel so that the reader is led through these juxtapositions to a full comprehension of the total grid of meaning.

The passage from Ecclesiastes begins with a calm, simple statement: ''One generation passeth away, and another generation cometh; but the earth abideth forever.'' (Hemingway was later to say that the hero of the novel was the earth, and his emphasis on the Spanish land, especially in the Burguete scene, sharpens that focus.) ''The sun also ariseth'' comes next and is followed by another list of harmonious natural elements: winds, rivers, the cyclic and returning patterns of seasonal movement. Considering the two epigraphs in tandem, no reader could stay focused for long on the ''lost generation'' image. The tone of the second epigraph is clearly positive; it comes second; it is much longer; it maintains its dominance.

During this period of his writing life, Hemingway was much interested in the *sound* of prose. He and John Dos Passos, a close friend who was also a novelist and travel writer, read aloud to each other from the Bible, particularly the Old Testament. The resonance, the incantatory rhythms, the sheer drama of the language in the King James version were in some ways a model for Hemingway's own writing. Though he was not rhetorical in the same ways, he understood the value of an incremental style. He consistently built his paragraphs, and his chapters, to achieve one overwhelming effect. Short sentences accenting longer ones, a vowel sound repeated subtly as well as obviously – in many ways Hemingway was conscious of the overall impact of his writing at every stage in a story or novel. The reader was at least partly led through a text by elements so carefully designed that their effect was unobtrusive.

So, Hemingway has worked hard to establish a contradiction from the very beginning of the novel. Is this a book about wastrels, the dregs of the postwar "meaninglessness," or is it about the eternally seeking person who wants to carve out a set of values and a notion of integrity on his or her own terms? Some critics saw only the former in *The Sun Also Rises*. For the author, however, changing the title of the book from *Fiesta* (which it had been called in draft and in its first published version in England) to its final form emphasized its positive characteristics. Jake Barnes and his friends – all of them – are a group because they share the same beliefs and experiences. Except for Robert Cohn, whose differences are less heinous than Jake sometimes thinks them to be, the displaced Americans and Britons are moving through a festival period in their lives, punctuating their aimless existence abroad with an organized visit to Spain for the bullfights. For Jake Barnes, who is a journalist in Paris, this trip is his vacation. The fiesta atmosphere, then, and the unusual behavior of the characters are not the everyday canvas of their lives. It is as if Hemingway is suggesting that even on vacation, even far from the social coercions and normal contexts for their behavior, these characters manage to stay in control – even if sometimes on the ragged edge of control.

The organization of the novel shows how central Jake Barnes is to his community of friends. A key theme is the notion of community: These are people who understand each other, the rules they live by, and the reasons for their choices. Only someone outside that community will have difficulty with the social code. Count

Mippipopolous may be a stranger to the group, but he understands the code and fits into the society. Robert Cohn, although he spends much time with the members of the group and thinks himself a special friend of both Jake and Brett, never manages to assimilate the rules. Jake, however, is clearly in charge – of the plans, the guest list, the activities, and the emotional nuance. He is the apparent hero of the novel, and his approval or disapproval sets the pattern for the other characters' reactions to things.

Hemingway had long been playing with the idea of creating a masterful new hero to counter the use of an antihero, or no hero at all, in much modern writing. (The *negative hero* Edith Wharton speaks about was so pervasive that the concept of the *hero* itself was almost a parody.) What he wasn't sure about was the method of expressing that heroism in such a way that the character and the context would be believable to modern readers. He had read Joyce's *Ulysses* in draft. Eliot's *The Waste Land,* with its characters of the fertile Fisher King – who has the power to bring dead lands back to life – and the modern men who are only shadows of the former kingly figures, was another important source for him. Sherwood Anderson had shown the literary world how to draw a strong male character who would seemingly play the role of the observer, but who in reality would be the central force for much of the action. And from Hemingway's reading of French and Russian writers, he had already seen how a character's psychological processes could be made to carry the freight of an entire novel.

Up to this point, however, Hemingway had been writing short stories, stories so short that editors hardly knew what to call them when they rejected them – sketches, vignettes perhaps, but not stories. In these (many of them collected in *In Our Time*), what hero there was never appeared in any heroic way. He too observed, avoided involvement, spoke seldom, and just as seldom acted decisively. When he was at war, as in the short interchapters of the book, he was a largely passive character. When he wrote about the bullfights, he was not even in the narrative.

The Sun Also Rises is in some ways an extension of the short stories in *In Our Time,* especially those that deal with war and with bullfighting. In the novel, the presence of the war is unescapable in the attitudes and conditions of the characters. We see nothing of

8

battle, although Jake and Bill's fishing expedition is a clear contrast to whatever turmoil they had experienced in wartime. We do see a great deal of bullfighting, and with good reason: The bullfight for Hemingway was a new source of ritual. Its participants and its observers understood the tradition; they could judge for themselves the quality, the excellence, of the action. Unlike postwar America, Spain was adept at maintaining its traditions. The bullfight became a paradigm for the religious beliefs so shaken in the Western world; it was a religious rite, a "tragedy in three acts," as Hemingway called it, and the matador was as Christlike as any modern person could hope to become. He took on dangers unheard of except in wartime; he survived, helped in part by the ritual itself, the other participants, and the community of the bullring. The bullfight became a microcosm of the good world — one with established and sensible rules, honor, bravery, and a higher purpose — just as the matador became a paradigm of a hero. The war had created a culture without heroes (or if we are to find them among Jake and his friends, the word "hero" must be redefined). In the bullring, in contrast, heroes abounded.

Accordingly, Hemingway divided the novel between Jake Barnes and Pedro Romero. In fact, when he began the book, in late July 1925 (he had written a chapter during the Pamplona trip), it opened with the bullfighter, then called Niño. There are thirty-one pages that begin, "I saw him for the first time in his room at the Hotel Pamplona." The story then shifts to a retrospective point of view, with the narrator explaining that he and his friends had agreed that Niño was the best torero they had seen, that his style was "the finest and purest," that he was "a great one."[9] The ostensible plot of this early section consists of the ambassador and his party inviting Niño to dinner with them and Jake protecting the young matador by not delivering the invitation. The attention stays on Niño. Brett is among the friends he meets, but the scene is much less charged with sexual tension than it is in the novel as we know it.

If Niño/Romero becomes the focal point of the book by appearing at the beginning, the importance of Jake and his friends becomes secondary. They are all observers. Jake achieves prominence in the group because he is the aficionado, and in this early draft he is able to protect Niño from the voracious American party. But Hemingway did not really know the life of Spanish bull-fighters, so such an exclusive focus would have been difficult to maintain.

His next version of the novel opened with a long description of Lady Brett Ashley, intertwined with characterizations of Jake Barnes. "This is a novel about a lady. Her name is Lady Ashley and when the story begins she is living in Paris and it is Spring. That should be a good setting for a romantic but highly moral story."[10] Brett's marital history, with all of its brutality, occupies the second paragraph of the first chapter, and Hemingway works hard – perhaps too hard – at creating sympathy for her. She is clearly a positive, brave, imaginative, and loving heroine who is just as clearly the victim of war in numerous ways. The second half of the chapter is occupied with Mike Campbell, who is also positively presented.

Chapter II introduces Jake Barnes as the narrator. In his direct explanation of his role in the novel (as a "detached narrator" as well as Mr. Jake Barnes), Hemingway tries to use that mocking, quasi-humorous tone that he chooses for his *Esquire* columns during the 1930s, for *Green Hills of Africa,* and for some of his stories. It may not work, but it testifies to his intuition that making Jake palatable for readers might be difficult. This is the opening of Chapter II in the earlier version:

> I did not want to tell this story in the first person but I find that I must. I wanted to stay well outside of the story so that I would not be touched by it in any way, and handle all the people in it with that irony and pity that are so essential to good writing. I even thought I might be amused by all the things that are going to happen to Lady Brett Ashley and Mr. Robert Cohn and Michael Campbell, Esq., and Mr. Jake Barnes. But I made the unfortunate mistake, for a writer, of first having been Mr. Jake Barnes. So it is not going to be splendid and cool and detached after all. "What a pity!" as Brett used to say.
>
> "What a pity!" was a little joke we all had. Brett was having her portrait painted by a very rich American . . .
>
> So my name is Jacob Barnes and I am writing the story, not as I believe is usual in these cases, from a desire for confession, because being a Roman Catholic I am spared that Protestant urge to literary production, nor to set things all out the way they happened for the

good of some future generation, nor any other of the usual highly
moral urges, but because I believe it is a good story.
I am a newspaper man living in Paris. . . .[11]

He goes on to explain (and he repeats in a later chapter) that he is
passionately in love with Brett and that he cannot live without her
when she is near.

Present-day readers of *The Sun Also Rises* do not have any of this
information. The novel begins with Robert Cohn and his boxing
history, and because we are perhaps accustomed to having primary characters introduced first, Hemingway's opening with Robert
may give us a slightly twisted impression. Even though the author's tone is wry, isn't Cohn a key figure? What is his role in the
novel, and why does Hemingway finally begin the book with him
and not with Romero or Brett, or even with Jake?

Literary history is full of stories of changes made in manuscripts
at the suggestion of some editor or friend. In Hemingway's case
(and this being his first novel, he may have been less confident
than he liked to pretend), he had given the manuscript to his
friend F. Scott Fitzgerald to read. Fitzgerald was an established
author; he had been earning his living by writing fiction for five or
six years, and his 1925 novel *The Great Gatsby* had been a monumental critical success. It was modern writing as Hemingway
knew and admired it. So when Fitzgerald suggested that Hemingway was writing badly throughout the first chapter and a half (the
section devoted to Brett, Mike, and Jake), Hemingway simply cut
out the beginning. It was already in galley proofs. Changing it
would have been costly, even if Hemingway had known exactly
how to make the changes.

What Fitzgerald objected to were the "careless and ineffectual"
parts, a tone of "condescending casuallness [sic]" in the opening.
He listed for several pages, sentences and events that must be
changed and then concluded, "from p. 30 I began to like the novel
but Ernest I can't tell you the sense of disappointment that beginning with its elephantine facetiousness gave me. Please do what
you can about it in proof. It's 7500 words — you could reduce it to
5000."[12]

Faced with such a list and such hearty condemnation, Hemingway was evidently unable to handle the editing and paring. The

11

changes he did make probably surprised Fitzgerald, who certainly had not told him to cut the section altogether (he had simply suggested that it be reduced by a third). The resultant shift in emphasis, then, from Brett, Mike, and Jake to Robert Cohn, was possibly an unintentional result of Hemingway's desperate attempt to clean up the opening of the novel. Beginnings, after all, were crucial; the reader might not stay with the book until page 30.

Hemingway's cutting may have changed the reader's initial impression in such a way as to blur the real lines of the novel. Or, looked at more charitably, the focus on Cohn was a brilliant "new" way of bringing the reader into the text by focusing on a secondary character. If the modern novel was to involve readers by keeping them guessing about the alignment of characters, the significance of scenes, even the real direction of the plot, then *The Sun Also Rises* was an important example of that change in method.

Favorable critics saw the novel as a totality, its opening planned to lead innovatively into an unexpected story. Only Hemingway may have known how misleading his opening was; only Hemingway may have been surprised at the generally good critical reception of the book by sophisticated modern readers. And that was the audience Hemingway cared about.

The Sun Also Rises, in fact, was considered a new manifesto of modernist style and was praised for its dialogue and its terse, objective presentation of characters. Hemingway was delighted. He had known that his stories were what he wanted, that they were important fiction, but this reception of his first attempt at a novel (not including his ten-day effort, *Torrents of Spring,* written as a parody of Sherwood Anderson's novel *Dark Laughter*) surprised him. He had written the first version of *The Sun Also Rises* between July and September 1925 and had spent the next winter revising it.[13]

His letters are peppered with comments about how hard he was working, how difficult good writing was, how much he enjoyed it when it went right. Part of the modernist aesthetic was that writing was so satisfying that it replaced other kinds of satisfaction, and yet the moral imperative that one work — the Puritan ethic of hard work — rings clear throughout Hemingway's apprenticeship years. His attention to detail, to word choice, to paragraph development, to the voice and perspective of each scene, is obvious in the artistry of the novel, much as it had been in the stories he had already published.

We have seen the way Hemingway made major changes to the text – at least to the early chapters. There are countless other changes – some slight, some more critical – throughout the manuscript, and part of Hemingway's greatness as a writer stems from the accuracy of his artistic judgment. He is his own best editor. Here are three examples of his editing. Early in the novel, he makes subtle changes in the relationship between Cohn and Jake. During the first scene in Jake's office, when Cohn is talking about going to South America, Hemingway encourages us to have sympathy for Cohn. In draft, this scene in the manuscript has an extra paragraph (here underlined):

> "No; listen, Jake. If I handled both our expenses, would you go to South America with me?"
> "Why me?"
> <u>He was quite frank and artless. That was what was nice about him.</u>
> "You can talk Spanish. And it would be more fun with two of us." (p. 10).

Not only is Cohn presented with rather more dignity here, but Jake appears more flip than he is in the published text. When Cohn asks, "Aren't you working?" Jake replies, in the manuscript version, "No. <u>I just come down here for fun.</u>" And in the following passage, when Jake deflates Cohn's romantic view of the bar, the manuscript version has Jake just agreeing. In the published version, he substantially refutes Cohn's enthusiasm.

Published Version	*Manuscript Version*
"This is a good place," he said.	"This is a good place," he said.
"There's a lot of liquor," I agreed.	"It's a nice place," I agreed.[14]

The same kind of deft change is evident in the scene in which Brett comes to Jake's room and then leaves again with the Count. In manuscript, the dialogue goes like this:

> We kissed good night and Brett shivered. "I'd better go," she said.
> "Good night, darling."

"Please stay," I said.
"No."

By the time the novel was published, the concluding exchange had become "You don't have to go" on Jake's part and "Yes" from Brett. Here she is agreeing with his negative, and somehow that makes her refusal to stay less threatening than it is in the earlier version.

The Hemingway Archive, the collection of Hemingway's manuscripts and correspondence housed in the John F. Kennedy Library in Boston, also contains several stories and sketches from the summer of 1925, the period when Hemingway was writing this novel. One is a story of Hemingway as house husband, caring for their puppy (and everything about the house) while Hadley is ill. Frustrated by the incessant household chores, he laments not being able to write about all of his experiences in Pamplona: "by the time the housework was done it was all gone."[15] There is also an account of a trip to Spain made with Mac and Mike Strater, complete with maps drawn on restaurant napkins and the correct pronunciation of Castilian Spanish. There are pieces of dialogue with Duff Twysden that didn't go into the novel, pieces that Hemingway worked from in creating Brett's speeches. In one of these Duff complains that everyone points her out in bars now that the novel has been published. There is also a note to the reader about the twenty-five pages cut out of the beginning of the book, jocularly explaining that it was worth giving up the early Hemingway descriptions of Brett to avoid the parallel descriptions of Jake/the author.[16]

One question that occurs when one consults the manuscript collection and attempts to fit together all of the changes and leftover fragments is why Hemingway made the choices he did. As Frederic Svoboda points out in his study of these manuscript versions, Hemingway shows his great skill "in his ability to integrate and interrelate all the varied elements of the novel, subordinating each to the overall effects he aimed to achieve, emphasizing or playing down each as his material required, but never losing sight of the whole."[17] It is the impact of the novel as a whole that creates its readership and its reputation. But the writer's choices

14

(whether or not he has a good "shit detector," in Hemingway's words) make the novel work as a totality. Hemingway at the beginning of the writing process, when he still saw *The Sun Also Rises* as the story of Spanish bullfights, or at a later stage, when the book was briefly titled *The Lost Generation*, did not know what the eventual texture and shape of the book would be. As it grew, as it became what it was going to become, choices made earlier had to be modified; new choices became necessary. To write about a group of people going on holiday in Spain is to write one kind of novel. *The Sun Also Rises* grew into a very different kind of book.

The modern American novel asked that readers invest themselves in helping to create the fiction. It was an open, suggestive structure, built from clusters of images and shaded descriptions as much as from plot, characters, and a linear progression of events. It demanded the same kind of close attention a good reader would give to poetry. As T. S. Eliot had said of Djuna Barnes's fiction, "a prose that is altogether alive demands something of the reader that the ordinary novel reader is not prepared to give."[18] The fact that so many readers have been willing to give such careful, even rapt, attention to Hemingway's writing has made him one of the key American modernists. There is no question about his influence, his example to writers both American and foreign, his major role in changing fiction from a representation of life to a recreation of it, even a replacement for it. Hemingway's power lay in imagining a world so entirely, so accurately, that readers believed in its existence. His monumental simplicity – each word fitted into place for maximum effect and chosen from a vocabulary that would reach the least able reader – set writing on a new track, one accessible to the limited reader but equally rich and suggestive for the most sophisticated. Hemingway was the master of control in the technique of writing.

He was also the master of presentation of the scenes of life, episodes so apparently true, so germane to his readers' experiences that no one questioned their authenticity. Because readers believed that Hemingway was indeed writing truly, and about important things, they read his work carefully. Their belief in him and his art gave his fiction credibility. If a story seemed to be unfocused or fragmentary, the writer giving just a hint of the action or characterization, readers supplied the rest; they came to Hemingway's fiction willing to adjust their sights, to clarify for themselves the perceptions so deftly conveyed. Turning the focus control, as on a telescope or gunsight, the reader moved into line, worked to make the angle right; and the magical involvement of reader with text was achieved. "I sometimes think my style is suggestive rather than direct. The reader must often use his imagination or lose the most subtle part of my thought," Hemingway wrote late in his life.[19]

When Hemingway wrote *The Sun Also Rises,* he was trying to make a clear statement about his life, his friends, his rebellion against the codifying temper of the postwar years in America. Like many writers and artists, he objected to the legislation of morals that Prohibition, the resurgence of all-American feeling, and the rebirth of the Ku Klux Klan suggested. His depiction of the anguish inherent in leaving the familiar – family, country, lifestyle – is not lost in the gaiety and rancor of the expatriate experience; in fact, it gives the novel some of its resonance. There are many reasons for these characters' unhappiness. To dwell on "irony and pity" is just a pastime; the real issues are the lack of alignment between profession and occupation, between lovers, between vacation and work, between ideals of Spain and France, between nature and the commercial. As full of disjunctures as a picture puzzle, *The Sun Also Rises* still presents a story whole, its fragments necessarily scattered throughout the narrative, and readers accept the fragmentation as one of the marks of Hemingway's truth. They seize on the purity of Pedro Romero, the wit of the bemused Mike Campbell, the taciturn acceptances of Jake Barnes, the flip bravado of Brett Ashley as the symbols of the characters who survive the onslaught of real life.

The essays collected here attempt to bring to the reading of this novel new perspectives, new views of a book that will continue to be read during the remainder of this century, even though its contemporaneity should have diminished long ago. "Literature is news that stays news," Ezra Pound said nearly seventy years ago.[20] The varied readings of this 1926 novel, all just now completed – nearly sixty years after the book's first publication – prove

Hemingway's accomplishment. Scott Donaldson shows how much comedy the novel included and how that strain complemented the ostensibly heavier tone of the book. Michael S. Reynolds continues Donaldson's emphasis on placing the novel in its own historical context and ends by *re*covering the ground, much of which has been either lost or inaccurately remembered. Wendy Martin's reassessment of Brett Ashley bridges history and feminist critical stances, and Cathy N. Davidson and Arnold E. Davidson upset many established critical perspectives on the novel by providing a rich deconstructive analysis of important narrative issues. A retrospective essay, "Afterthoughts on the Twenties and *The Sun Also Rises*," by John W. Aldridge closes the collection. The reader will find disagreement among the essayists, and some major points of contention link essay to essay. The whole provides even further evidence of the brilliance, and the lasting evocativeness, of Hemingway's first novel and its memorable characters.

NOTES

1. "Hemingway Seems Out of Focus in the 'Sun Also Rises,'" *Chicago Daily Tribune*, November 27, 1926, p. 13; "Briefer Mention," anon. column in *The Dial* 82 (January 1927):73. Earlier citations from "Study in Futility," *Cincinnati Enquirer*, October 30, 1926, p. 5.

2. *Chicago Daily Tribune* review, p. 13; see Hemingway's letter to his mother, Grace Hall Hemingway, February 5, 1927, in *Ernest Hemingway: Selected Letters, 1917–1961*, ed. Carlos Baker (New York: Scribners, 1981), p. 243.

3. Edwin Muir, Review of *Fiesta* (British title of *The Sun Also Rises*), *Nation & Athenaeum* 41 (July 2, 1927):450, 452.

4. Chase, "Out of Little, Much," *Saturday Review of Literature* 3 (December 11, 1926):420–1; Gorman, "Hemingway Keeps His Promise," *The New York World*, November 14, 1926, p. 10M; and Rascoe, "Diversity in the Younger Set," *New York Sun*, November 6, 1929, p. 10.

5. Ford Madox Ford, "Some American Expatriates," *Vanity Fair* 28 (April 1, 1927):64, 98; Edmund Wilson, "The Sportsman's Tragedy," *New Republic* 53 (December 14, 1927):102–3; Hugh Walpole, "Contemporary American Letters," *Nation & Athenaeum* 41 (June 4, 1927):302–3.

6. N. L. Rothman, "Hemingway Whistles in the Dark," *The Dial* 84 (April 1, 1928):336–8; H. L. Mencken, review of *Men Without Women, American Mercury* 14 (May 1928):127.
7. Ezra Pound, "Small Magazines," *The English Journal* 19, no. 9 (November 1930):700. For a full description of this important relationship, see my *Hemingway and Faulkner: inventors/masters* (Metuchen, N.J.: Scarecrow Press, 1975).
8. Item 202c in the Hemingway Collection, John F. Kennedy Library. See also Carlos Baker, *Ernest Hemingway, A Life Story* (New York: Scribners, 1969), and Bernard Sarason, *Hemingway and the Sun Set* (Washington, D.C.: Microcard Editions, 1972).
9. Item 193, Hemingway Archive, John F. Kennedy Library.
10. From the Kennedy Collection, as reprinted in Appendix B, Frederic Joseph Svoboda, *Hemingway and The Sun Also Rises, The Crafting of a Style* (Lawrence: University Press of Kansas, 1983), pp. 131–3.
11. Ibid. Svoboda's tables of correlations and versions of the manuscript, as well as his deductions in the text proper, are useful to any reader of this novel.
12. Ibid., pp. 137–9.
13. See Baker, *A Life;* Svoboda, *Crafting of a Style;* and *Letters,* p. 198, April 1, 1926, where he tells Perkins that the manuscript will be mailed in a couple of weeks ("The Sun Also Rises will go to the typist to be retyped and then I'll send it to you").
14. Item 193, Hemingway Archive, John F. Kennedy Library.
15. Item 409A, Hemingway Archive, ibid.
16. Items 530, 546.5, and 202d, Hemingway Archive, ibid.
17. Svoboda, *Crafting of a Style,* p. 114.
18. T. S. Eliot, "Introduction" to *Nightwood; The Selected Works of Djuna Barnes* (New York: Farrar, Straus, Cudahy, 1962), p. 228.
19. Hemingway writing in *Playboy,* as collected in *The Uncollected Prose of Ernest Hemingway,* ed. Clinton Burhans (East Lansing: Michigan State University Press, 1967), p. 692.
20. Ezra Pound, "Vorticism," *Fortnightly Review* 96 (September 1, 1914):469.

2

Humor in *The Sun Also Rises*

SCOTT DONALDSON

1

E RNEST Hemingway started out trying to be funny. On the evidence of his high school compositions, a classmate recalled, "one might have predicted that he would be a writer of humor."[1] In the *Trapeze,* the Oak Park and River Forest Township high school weekly newspaper, he made fun of himself, his sister, his friends, and the school itself. Some of these pieces were fashioned after the epistolary subliteracy of Ring Lardner's *You Know Me, Al* (1916). "Well Sue as you are the editor this week I thot as how I would write and tell you about how successful I was with my editorials so you would be cheered up and feel how great a responsibility you have in swaying the public opinions." He had written "a hot editorial" on "Support the Swimming Team" and expected at least 500 people at the next meet, "and do you know how many guys there was there?" Only one, and he "never read no editorials."[2] Parody also figured in contributions to the *Trapeze;* from the beginning, Hemingway understood how to take an elevated, formal pattern and bring it crashing to earth.

> Lives of football men remind us,
> We can dive and kick and slug.
> And departing leave behind us,
> Hoof prints on another's mug.[3]

In his juvenile fiction, too, he was working for laughs. One of his three published high school stories, "A Matter of Colour," does nothing but build up to a punch line delivered by and somewhat at the expense of a stolid Swede.[4]

After brief tours with the Kansas City *Star* and the ambulance

19

service on the Italian front during World War I, Hemingway came back to Chicago, landed a job writing booster copy for the *Cooperative Commonwealth,* and in his spare time experimented with humor. He fired off satirical rewrites of world news to *Vanity Fair,* which fired them right back. He also concocted mock advertising campaigns to entertain his friends. One involved bottling stockyard blood as "Bull Gore for Bigger Babies." Another, rather less surprising today than in 1920, ridiculed the "current Interchurch World campaign to sell Christianity in paid-for space."[5] Together with Bill Horne and Y. K. Smith, he put together thirteen verses of the doggerel "Battle of Copenhagen," its humor aimed at ethnic groups.

> Ten tribes of red Pawnees
> Were sulking behind trees
> at the Battle of Copenhagen.
>
> Three thousand greasy Greeks
> Arrayed in leathern breeks
> And smelling strongly of leeks
> at the Battle of Copenhagen.
>
> A half a million Jews
> Ran back to tell the news
> of the Battle of Copenhagen.[6]

Jewish jokes, especially, were part of Hemingway's heritage. At school he was called Hemingstein, apparently because he was careful in money matters, and rather enjoyed the nickname.

When he caught on with the Toronto *Daily Star* and *Star Weekly,* first as a freelancer in 1920 and then as a regular feature writer and correspondent from early 1921 until the end of 1923, Hemingway found a commercial outlet for his brand of comedy. As *Star Weekly* editor J. Herbert Cranston put it, "Hemingway . . . could write in good, plain Anglo-Saxon, and had a certain much prized gift of humor."[7] His earliest pieces for the paper dealt with such subjects as a shaky-kneed visit to a barber college for a free shave, a politician totally ignorant of the sport who appeared at prizefights to curry favor with the voters, and the disastrous consequences of believing the promotional copy issued by summer vacation resorts. Later, during nearly two years as a roving European correspondent based in Paris, Hemingway derided the empty life of do-nothing expatriates and refused to be impressed by the supposedly great men he encountered at conferences in Lausanne and Genoa. The watchword was "irreverence," the target all received wisdom. The attitude most commonly struck was that of the "wise guy," and as Delmore Schwartz pointed out, it was in this role that Hemingway first made an impression. "To be a wise guy," Schwartz wrote, "is to present an impudent, aggressive, knowing, and self-possessed face or 'front' to the world. The most obvious mark of the wise guy is his sense of humor which expresses his scorn and his sense of independence; he exercises it as one of the best ways of controlling a situation and of demonstrating his superiority to all situations."[8]

That description well suits the Hemingway feature for the *Star Weekly* entitled "Our Confidential Vacation Guide," with descriptions such as this:

> Beautiful Lake Flyblow nestles like a plague spot in the heart of the great north woods. All around it rise the majestic hills. Above it towers the majestic sky. On every side of it is the majestic shore. The shore is lined with majestic dead fish − dead of loneliness.[9]

The wise guy pose also pervades "Condensing the Classics," an August 1921 venture into Shrinklits that reduced great novels and poems to a headline and a lead paragraph. Among the headlines were "Crazed Knight in Weird Tilt," "Big Cat in Flames," "Albatross Slayer Flays Prohibition," and "Slays His White Bride − Society Girl, Wed to African War-Hero, Found Strangled in Bed."[10] And it explains the irreverence with which Hemingway dismissed Benito Mussolini as the biggest bluff in Europe and the Russian foreign minister Tchitcherin as a homosexual dandy. Sometimes his journalistic humor was good-natured or high-spirited; more often it was satirical, with a target firmly in mind. As that satirical bent was translated into Hemingway's fiction, it became clear that no target was sacrosanct. His first fictional publication as a professional writer, the May 1922 two-page fable for *The Double Dealer* called "A Divine Gesture," employed irony and dark humor in depicting an indifferent God and trivial human beings.

When Hemingway left the newspaper business at the end of 1923, he had been turning out amusing copy for so long that he naturally tended to think of himself as a humorist.[12] The wise guy strain of that humor led directly to *The Torrents of Spring,* the satiric novella he dashed off between drafts of *The Sun Also Rises* in November 1925. Like much of Hemingway's juvenilia, *Torrents* was a parody. Its victim was Sherwood Anderson, and particularly Anderson's novel *Dark Laughter,* which had appeared earlier in the year. In that book, Anderson celebrated the wisdom and virtue of the unlettered primitive and indulged in a good deal of obtrusive philosophical musing. Anderson had earlier helped to introduce Hemingway to the literary world of Paris, but in *Torrents* the young writer relentlessly exposed the failings of his benefactor, while also making sport of expatriation, literature with a capital L, Scott Fitzgerald, and Gertrude Stein.

Individual passages are very funny indeed. Scripps O'Neil, a Harvard graduate and would-be writer with two wives and minimal brain power, masquerades as the hero. He comes to a railway depot bearing the sign PETOSKEY in large letters. "Scripps read the sign again. Could this be Petoskey?" He comes across another sign advertising BROWN'S BEANERY THE BEST BY TEST. "Was this, after all, Brown's Beanery?" he wonders. He goes to a pump factory to get a job. "Could this really be a pump factory?" He walks up to a door with "a sign on it: KEEP OUT. THIS MEANS YOU. Can this mean me? Scripps wondered."[13] But the whole of *The Torrents of Spring* adds up to less than the sum of its sometimes hilarious parts. The humor is almost always at someone's expense; the characters are insignificant, the plot fantastic, the theme invisible. *Torrents* runs to only about one hundred pages and could profitably have been cut to half that length.

Thirty years later, when his own work became the butt of various parodies, Hemingway renounced the genre. "Parodies," he told A. E. Hotchner, "are what you write when you are associate editor of the Harvard *Lampoon.* . . . The step up from writing parodies is writing on the wall above the urinal."[14] The step he himself took in late 1925 and early 1926 was to rewrite the novel that most successfully incorporated his gift for hu.nor. The epigraph to *The Torrents of Spring,* from Fielding, declares that "the only source of the true Ridiculous (as it appears to me) is affectation."[15] When Hemingway finished *Torrents* to take up *The Sun Also Rises* again, he was keenly aware of the affected and the pretentious in all their forms, but he subordinated the wise guy, satiric vein in his novel. In its place Hemingway achieved in *Sun* "a delicate balance of ridicule and affection"[16] that contributes to character development and underscores the theme. The humor turns bitter as the novel progresses, but it does not start that way and the bitterness is earned, not gratuitous.

2

Hemingway announced *The Sun Also Rises* with an inside joke. The two epigraphs — one from "GERTRUDE STEIN *in conversation,*" the other from Ecclesiastes — are linked together rhetorically. "You are all a lost generation," Stein said, and in the Bible the preacher said, "One generation passeth away, and another generation cometh; but the earth abideth forever. . . . The sun also ariseth." Once one knows the provenance of Stein's remark, it is impossible to take it as seriously as the biblical passage. In *A Moveable Feast,* written thirty years later, Hemingway told the story as he remembered it. Stein had had some trouble with her Ford, and the young garageman who tried to repair it did not do a good job. Chastising him, the garage owner said, "You are all a génération perdue," and Stein appropriated his comment in talking to Hemingway. "That's what you all are," she told him, referring to the young people who had served in the war. "You have no respect for anything. You drink yourselves to death. . . . You're all a lost generation, just exactly as the garage keeper said." When he wrote his first novel, Hemingway added, he "tried to balance Miss Stein's quotation from the garage keeper with one from Ecclesiastes," but he did not agree with her about the particular lostness of his generation: "all generations were lost by something and always had been and always would be."[17]

It is not surprising that Hemingway, in writing *A Moveable Feast,* recalled the anecdote rather differently than he did on September 27, 1925, when he set it down as a foreword to the novel-in-progress he then intended to call *The Lost Generation.* The scene is the garage once again, but as it happens, the young mechanic who fixes Stein's car does an excellent job, and she asks the garage

23

owner where he finds boys to work so well. She'd heard that one couldn't get them to work anymore. He has no trouble with the young boys of 1925, the garageman says. He's taken and trained them himself. "It is the ones between twenty-two and thirty that are no good. C'est un génération perdu.* No one wants them. They are no good. They were spoiled. The young ones, the new ones are all right again." There are two very different things in this earlier version of the "lost generation" story. First, Stein does not generalize from the garageman's remark. Second and more important, instead of denying the uniqueness of his generation, Hemingway goes on to insist upon it: "this generation that is lost has nothing to do with any Younger generation about whose outcome much literary speculation occurred in times past. This is not a question of what kind of mothers will flappers make or where is bobbed hair leading us [the sorts of subjects addressed by the Fitzgeralds in magazine articles]. This is about something that is already finished. For whatever is going to happen to the generation of which I am a part has already happened." No matter what future entanglements or complications or promised salvations occur, "none of it will matter particularly to this generation because to them the things that are given to people to happen have already happened."[18]

This foreword of Hemingway's was later cut, of course, and Stein's remark stands on the page without elaboration, unless you happen to read *A Moveable Feast* or Item 202c in the Hemingway Archive at the Kennedy library in Boston. But the private joke — that Stein's aphorism came originally from the lips of a French garage owner and that it is his voice, not that of the pontifical Stein, that is juxtaposed to the eternal Word — could not have escaped Hemingway's consciousness as he was working on *The Sun Also Rises*. In fact, the dual epigraphs suggest the complicated nature of the book's tone, an intricate mixture of humorous and serious elements. This tone shifts according to which character is speaking. *The Sun Also Rises* runs heavily to dialogue, and the characters reveal themselves largely through what they do and

---

*Hemingway uses the feminine form in his preface to *The Sun Also Rises* and this form in *A Moveable Feast*.

24

say, with only occasional interpretive suggestions from the narrator. Most of these characters are capable of producing merriment in others, whether or not they intend to do so. But what is remarkable is how different their kinds of humor are and how they are distinguished from each other in this way.

Hemingway had an excellent ear for talk, and much that is funny in *The Sun Also Rises* depends on that gift. Consider, for instance, the pidgin English of Count Mippipopolous, which features the rugged Anglo-Saxon verb "got," does not discriminate between tenses, and shows a knack for choosing almost the right word. "You got class all over you," he tells Brett. "You got the most class of anybody I ever seen." "Nice of you," she responds. "Mummy would be pleased." As for himself, he gets more value for his money in old brandy, he says "than in any other antiquities." "Got many antiquities?" Brett inquires. "I got a houseful." Though hardly a native speaker of English, the count is perceptive enough to note Brett's clipped manner of speech. "When you talk to me, you never finish your sentences at all," he complains. Jake also notices this linguistic trait: "The English spoken language — the upper classes, any way — must have fewer words than the Eskimo," and this is amply illustrated in the conversation of Lady Ashley and Mike Campbell (58, 62, 149).

This early conversation delineates Brett's rather wry manner and the count's serious attention (he never "jokes" anyone, he insists) to enjoying the best things in life: beautiful women and objects, good food and drink. Moreover, the discussion foreshadows certain questions that the novel eventually confronts. What constitutes "class" in human behavior? Do the count's "values" suffice? And, of course, it does these things in the context of humor deriving from the gulf between the subjects under examination — rare antiques, social position, ethical standards — and the count's tough, unlettered speech.

Belaboring the origins of humor is notoriously unrewarding. There used to be a course in comedy at Yale that the undergraduates critiqued, quite rightly, as "English 63. Comedy. 63 dollars worth of books and not a laugh in the course." Still, it needs to be observed that Hemingway's humor in *The Sun Also Rises*, like that in the Count Mippopopolous–Brett Ashley exchange, usually depends on what the philosopher Paul Morreall calls "incongruity of presentation."[19] "Hemingway's primary technique of humor," as Sheldon Grebstein observed in his fine treatment of the subject, "is that of incongruous juxtaposition," among other things the juxtaposition of "highbrow speech against the vulgate."[20] Working with word play – verbal slips, puns, double entendre – James Hinkle recently located some sixty jokes embedded in the novel.[21] But there is more to it than word play, for Hemingway plays with ideas as well as words, adopting an incongruous point of view, confusing categories, violating logical principles, and so forth. The precise technique varies from character to character, and some characters are a good deal funnier than others.

Jake Barnes tells the story of *The Sun Also Rises* so unobtrusively and convincingly that it never occurs to us to challenge his view of events, as for instance we tend to do with that of Frederic Henry in *A Farewell to Arms*. Jake deserves sympathy because of his wound. But he wins our trust primarily because of his capacity to assess human behavior with objectivity. Like the prototypical newspaperman he has few illusions about anyone, including himself. So he adopts a posture of irony, one that moves from a good-natured sarcasm at the beginning of the novel to a biting, bitterly sardonic strain at the end.

In Chapter III Jake picks up a streetwalker and takes her to dinner "because of a vague sentimental idea that it would be nice to eat with some one." But the girl objects to the place he takes her. "This is no great thing of a restaurant." "No," Jake admits. "Maybe you would rather go to Foyot's. Why don't you keep the cab and go on?" (16). He takes a rather cynical view of the political and journalistic professions as well:

> At eleven o'clock I went over to the Quai d'Orsay in a taxi and went in and sat with about a dozen correspondents, while the foreign-office mouthpiece, a young Nouvelle Revue Française diplomat in horn-rimmed spectacles, talked and answered questions for half an hour. . . . Several people asked questions to hear themselves talk and there were a couple of questions asked by news service men who wanted to know the answers. There was no news. (p. 36)

His concierge has social pretensions and wants to make sure that all of Jake's guests measure up to her standards. If they do not, she sends them away. It gets to the point where one friend, "an extremely underfed-looking painter," writes Jake a letter asking for "a pass to get by the concierge" (53).

Where his war wound is concerned, Jake obviously does not think it funny himself, but he is capable of seeing the humor in the way others react to it. He is particularly amused by the "wonderful speech" of the Italian liaison colonel who came to see him in the Ospedale Maggiore in Milano:

> "You, a foreigner, an Englishman" (any foreigner was an Englishman) "have given more than your life." What a speech! I would like to have it illuminated to hang in the office. He never laughed. He was putting himself in my place, I guess. "Che mala fortuna! Che mala fortuna!" (p. 31)

In conversation, the subject is taboo. He's "sick," Jake tells his poule (15–16). "Well, let's shut up about it," he tells Brett (26–7). When the count proposes that Jake and Brett get married, they collaborate on an evasive reply. "We want to lead our own lives," Jake says. "We have our careers," Brett chimes in (61). Twice Bill Gorton hovers on the brink of the forbidden subject. Why, he wonders, did Brett go to San Sebastian with Cohn? "Why didn't she go off with some of her own people? Or you? – he slurred that over – or me? Why not me?" Then, to break the awkwardness, Bill delivers a soliloquy on his own face in the shaving mirror. The next day, while they are fishing the Irati, Bill refers to the wound again in the course of satirizing the conventional stateside view of expatriation. According to this view, he tells Jake, expatriates like himself "don't work. One group claims women support you. Another group claims you're impotent."

"No," Jake responds forthrightly, "I just had an accident." But Bill shuns the topic. "Never mention that," he tells Jake. "That's the sort of thing . . . you ought to work up into a mystery. Like Henry's bicycle." The reference is to a rumored childhood injury that compromised the masculinity of Henry James, and it caused a good deal of consternation at Scribners before they allowed it to stand, stripped of the identifying surname. But in context, it allows Jake and Bill to guide their conversation in a related but less personally sensitive direction. The important thing to note is Jake's capacity to put himself in Bill's place here. Bill had been doing splendidly but then, Jake thinks, "I was afraid he thought he had hurt me with that crack about being impotent." So Jake takes the cue from Henry's bicycle to launch into an inane discussion of whether it was on two wheels or three, on a horse or in an airplane, that the Master suffered his injury. This leads to joysticks, though, and eventually Bill can only clear the air by telling Jake how fond he is of him (115–16).

It is not talk about his injury that most distresses Jake, of course, but the way it impairs his relationship with Brett. At the fiesta the high spirits of the fishing trip dissipate as Brett transforms the men around her into steers or swine. Cohn adopts an annoying air of superiority, then an equally annoying pose of suffering. Mike Campbell rides him unmercifully in attacks that Jake despises himself for enjoying. Brett further compromises his integrity by persuading him to take her to Pedro Romero. Eventually Jake's sardonic bent assumes a bitterness that inhibits rather than encourages laughter. "It seemed they were all such nice people," he reflects at mid-fiesta (146). On the last evening in Pamplona, after Brett has run off with Romero, Jake feels "low as hell" and drinks absinthe in an attempt to brighten his mood. "Well," Bill says, "it was a swell fiesta." "Yes," Jake answers, "something doing all the time" (222).

By the time he and Bill and Mike have parted, Jake Barnes is in the grip of a thoroughgoing cynicism. A few weeks earlier, he had rather enjoyed the count's unabashed cultivation of material pleasures:

> We dined at a restaurant in the Bois. It was a good dinner. Food had an excellent place in the count's values. So did wine. The count was in fine form during the meal. So was Brett. It was a good party. (p. 61)

During the fiesta, however, he learns how devastating it can be to stay on at a party with Brett. And he is reminded repeatedly by Cohn, by Campbell, and by Romero of his own incapacity to make love to the woman he loves. Food and drink and friendship are the pleasures left to him, but the first two have lost their savor, and it sometimes seems that all three must be purchased. Dining alone in Bayonne, he reflects witheringly on the materialism of the French:

Everything is on such a clear financial basis in France. It is the simplest country to live in. No one makes things complicated by becoming your friend for any obscure reason. If you want people to like you you have only to spend a little money. I spent a little money and the waiter liked me. He appreciated my valuable qualities. He would be glad to see me back. I would dine there again some time and he would be glad to see me, and would want me at his table. It would be a sincere liking because it would have a sound basis. I was back in France. (p. 233)

From that point to the end of the novel, Jake cannot enjoy human transactions. There is some healing benefit to be derived from diving into the ocean off San Sebastian, but at the hotel the corrupt bike riders are arranging who will win the following day and then the two wires from Lady Ashley arrive:

COULD YOU COME HOTEL MONTANA MADRID AM RATHER IN TROUBLE BRETT. (pp. 238–9)

And Jake must answer the call.

In Madrid, things go badly. Jake is nervous about leaving his bags downstairs at the somewhat seedy Hotel Montana. Perhaps it is true that the "personages" of the establishment are "rigidly selected," but nonetheless he "would welcome the upbringal" of his bags. As for Brett, she keeps insisting that she doesn't want to talk about her time with Romero, but she cannot resist going on about it. Jake becomes increasingly monosyllabic in response: "Yes." "Really?" "Good." "No." "Good." "Dear Brett." Then he proceeds to get drunk. At the Palace Hotel bar downtown, they each have three martinis before lunch. Aside from Romero, there is nothing to talk about. "Isn't it a nice bar?" Brett asks. "They're all nice bars," Jake answers. They have lunch at Botin's, where Jake eats "a very big meal" of roast young suckling pig and drinks three bottles of *rioja alta* (or is it five?) with little assistance from Brett. "Don't get drunk," she implores him. "Jake, don't get drunk." But there is not much else to be done, and it does not help when they take a ride and sit close to each other and Brett says, "Oh, Jake, we could have had such a damned good time together." The mounted policeman ahead raises his baton and the taxi slows suddenly, pressing Brett against him. "Yes," Jake says, "Isn't it pretty to think so?" (pp. 241–7). Hemingway tried that

29

closing line in two other ways — "It's nice as hell to think so" and "Isn't it nice to think so" — before settling on the bitter adjective "pretty" that exactly communicates Jake's despair.[22] Brett is going back to Mike, but for Jake there is no one, and no hope, and no humor.

At certain places in the first draft of the novel, Hemingway interchanged "I" and "Jake" tellingly; in fact, the parallels between author and character are marked enough for readers to suppose that for the most part Jake Barnes thinks and talks very much like Ernest Hemingway himself. Jake is a repository of those same ethnic and nationalistic prejudices, for instance, that often cropped up in Hemingway's juvenilia and journalism. Mrs. Braddocks, loud and rude, "was a Canadian and had all their easy social graces" (17). The German maitre d'hotel at Montoya's, nosy and knowing, is satisfactorily put in his place by Bill Gorton (209–11). The American ambassador and his circle exploit others for their amusement and are stupid into the bargain (171–2, 215).[23] The French are grasping (233). The Spanish, on the other hand, generously share their food, wine, and companionship (103–4, 156–7). Spanish peasants, significantly, cross the language barrier to express their good humor. The Basques who accompany Bill and Jake on the bus ride to Burguete offer them a drink from their big leather winebag. As Jake tips up the wineskin, one of the Basques imitates the sound of a klaxon motor horn so suddenly and surprisingly that Jake spills some of the wine. A few minutes later, he fools Jake with the klaxon again, and everyone laughs (103–4, 156–7).

Most of the ethnic humor in the book, however, is less good-natured and depends upon linguistic nuance. Robert Cohn is the butt of most of it. Some of the jibes against him are made by relatively minor characters. Harvey Stone and Jake are having a drink at the Select when Cohn comes up. "Hello, Robert," Stone says, "I was just telling Jake here that you're a moron" (43–4). Immediately thereafter Frances Clyne devastates Cohn at greater length, also in the presence of Jake. Frances satirically unveils Cohn's narcissism, his self-pity, his habit of buying himself out of entanglements, and his stinginess in doing so. "I do not know," Jake thinks, "how people could say such terrible things to Robert

Cohn. . . . Here it was, all going on right before me, and I did not even feel an impulse to try and stop it. And this was friendly joking to what went on later" (48–50). What went on later, at its worst, came in the form of Mike Campbell's increasingly unfunny insults at Pamplona. But the primary source of information about Cohn, and the group's attitude toward him, is Jake himself.

Jake artfully belittles Cohn throughout, but especially in the opening chapter. "Robert Cohn was once middleweight boxing champion of Princeton," the novel begins, and the depreciation follows at once. "Do not think that I am very much impressed by that as a boxing title, but it meant a lot to Cohn." A "very shy and thoroughly nice boy," Cohn did not use his skill to knock down any of those who were snooty to him, as a Jew, at Princeton. In the gym itself, however, he was overmatched once and "got his nose permanently flattened. This . . . gave him a certain satisfaction of some strange sort, and it certainly improved his nose." Jake never met anyone in Cohn's class at Princeton who remembered him. Having disposed of his college career, Barnes continues his demeaning account.

Though Robert Cohn was "a nice boy, a friendly boy, and very shy," Jake acknowledges, his experience at Princeton embittered him; he came out of it "with painful self-consciousness and the flattened nose, and was married by the first girl who was nice to him." Married by, not to. After siring three children in five years and losing most of the fifty thousand dollars his father had left him, Cohn had just made up his mind to leave his wife when she left him instead, running off "with a miniature-painter." A *miniature*-painter! Next, Cohn goes to California and buys his way into the editorship of a literary magazine, but it becomes too expensive and he has to give it up. Meanwhile, he has "been taken in hand by a lady who hoped to rise with the magazine. She was very forceful, and Cohn never had a chance of not being taken in hand." This is Frances, who does not love Cohn but wants to "get what there was to get while there was still something available" and then to marry him. She brings him to Europe, where she had been educated, though he "would rather have been in America." Cohn then produces a novel that was "not really such a bad novel as the critics later called it," and for the first time begins to think of

31

himself as attractive to women and able to assert himself with them. It is at this dangerous stage of his continuing adolescence that Cohn meets Brett Ashley, with her curves like the hull of a racing yacht. Gazing at her, Jake comments, he "looked a great deal as his compatriot must have looked when he saw the promised land. Cohn, of course, was much younger. But he had that look of eager, deserving expectation" (3–7, 22). The mode is obviously ridicule, and Cohn's subsequent behavior – particularly his romanticization of *his* affair with Brett, his air of superiority toward Jake and Bill on that score, and his excessive barbering – well merits ridicule. Still, the opening salvo pretty much settles his hash.

To his credit, at one stage in Pamplona it appears that Cohn may be achieving a new maturity. He has foolishly proclaimed that he might be bored at the bullfights. Afterward Bill and Mike kid him about that, and Cohn is able to laugh at himself. "No. I wasn't bored. I wish you'd forgive me that." Bill forgives him, but not the rivalrous Mike (165–6). He continues baiting Cohn until even Brett tells him to "shove it along" (165–6). From this stage on, and despite Cohn's outbreak of pugilistic violence, Mike supplants him as the villain of the piece. Moreover, Mike's descent can be accurately calibrated on the scale of humor.

On first introduction, Mike Campbell seems an engaging ne'er-do-well. He is more than a little drunk on arrival in Paris and Brett accurately introduces him to Bill Gorton as "an undischarged bankrupt," but he is so excited about seeing Brett again and so eagerly anticipatory about the night ahead that these shortcomings appear unimportant. "I say, Brett," he thrice tells her, "you *are* a lovely piece." And he asks Jake and Bill twice, "Isn't she a lovely piece?" To taunt him, Bill asks Mike to go along to the prizefight, but he and Brett have a date in mind. "I'm sorry I can't go," Mike says, and Brett laughs (79–80). When the group reassembles in Pamplona, Mike again works his vein of humorous repetition. Brett suggests that he tell the story of the time his horse bolted down Piccadilly, but Mike refuses. "I'll not tell that story. It reflects discredit on me." Well, she suggests, tell them about the medals. "I'll not. That story reflects great discredit upon me." Brett could easily tell it, he supposes. "She tells all the stories that reflect discredit on me." In the end, he tells the story himself, and it does indeed place him in an unfavorable light, for he had gotten drunk and given away someone else's war medals to some girls in a night club. "They thought I was hell's own shakes of a soldier" (135–6).

Once started, Mike persists in his self-depreciation. He went bankrupt, he says, two ways — "gradually and then suddenly." What brought it on, he observes in sentence fragments, were "Friends . . . — I had a lot of friends. False friends. Then I had creditors, too. Probably had more creditors than anybody in England" (136). Soon thereafter there is the one successful dinner at the fiesta, where both Bill and Mike were "very funny. . . . They were good together" (146). Mike's bantering becomes progressively more strident, however, as the drinking increases, Cohn continues to hang about in pursuit of his lady love (Mike's fiancée), and Brett herself becomes infatuated with Romero. Mike ventilates his outrage in a vicious assault on Cohn. "Why do you follow Brett around like a poor bloody steer? Don't you know you're not wanted? I know when I'm not wanted. Why don't you know when you're not wanted? You came down to San Sebastian where you weren't wanted, and followed Brett around like a bloody steer." Once started, Mike's invective is hard to stop. None of their friends at San Sebastian "would invite you" to come along, he tells Cohn. "You can't blame them hardly. Can you? I asked them to. They wouldn't do it. You can't blame them, now. Can you? Now answer me. Can you blame them? . . . I can't blame them, Can you blame them? Why do you follow Brett around?" (142). Here, Mike's talent for repetition is used to abuse another human being, and there is nothing funny about such scorn.

Similarly, his habit of *self*-disparagement also palls as his financial irresponsibility becomes more manifest. "Who cares if he is a damn bankrupt?" Bill objects after they are ejected from a Pamplona bar by some people Mike owes money to (189). The answer, finally, is that everyone cares. Mike's technique is to disarm criticism by accusing himself before others do so, but that does not always amuse. He won't go into the bullring for the morning *encierro* at Pamplona, he tells Edna, because it "wouldn't be fair to my creditors" (200). At the last meeting with Bill and Jake in

Biarritz, when it turns out that Mike is broke and cannot pay for the drinks he's gambled for at poker dice, and has spent all of Brett's money as well, Mike again touches the wound, but less amusingly this time. Bill proposes another drink. "Damned good idea," Mike says. "One never gets anywhere by discussing finances." Then, since they've rented a car for the day, Mike suggests that they "take a drive. It might do my credit good." They decide to drive down to Hendaye, though Mike remarks he hasn't "any credit along the coast" (230). Under the circumstances, Mike's attempts at humor invite contempt. It had been ethically dubious of him to savage Cohn. And, as Morreall points out, "it can also be morally inappropriate to laugh about one's own situation, if by doing so we are detaching ourselves from our own moral responsibilities."[24]

In a less blameworthy fashion, Brett makes fun of her own drunkenness and promiscuity. The count advises her to drink the Mumm's champagne slowly, and later she can get drunk. "Drunk? Drunk?" she replies (59). When Jakes brings his poule to the bal musette, Brett is amused by the supposed disrespect for her status as a pure woman. "It's an insult to all of us," she laughs. "It's in restraint of trade," she laughs again (22). Laughing at herself in this way serves, of course, to forestall any change in her reckless style of life. In this sense it is fitting that she go back to Mike, who is "so damned nice" and "so awful" and so much her "sort of thing" (243).

3

The most consistently funny character in *The Sun Also Rises* is Bill Gorton. Gorton is clearly modeled on the humorist Donald Ogden Stewart, who did in fact go to Pamplona in 1925 with the Hemingways, Harold Loeb, Bill Smith, Pat Guthrie, and Lady Duff Twysden. Stewart later characterized Hemingway's novel as almost reportorial in its fidelity to the events of the fiesta. He may have come to that judgment, which undervalues the book's artistry, largely as a consequence of recognizing so much of his own sometimes "crazy humor" (as he called it) in Bill Gorton's material. In fact Don Stewart, like Bill Gorton, was almost constitutionally incapable of not amusing people.[25] As Scott Fitzgerald said of him, he "could turn a Sunday school picnic into a public holiday."[26]

It was very much in character, then, for Hemingway to make Bill Gorton—Don Stewart the source of humor in the two most high-spirited chapters of the novel. These are Chapter VIII, where Bill and Jake go out to dinner in Paris, and Chapter XII, where they go fishing along the Irati. In the Paris chapter, Bill has only recently come to Europe and has just returned from a trip to Austria and Hungary. Gorton is described as "very happy." His last book had sold well. He's excited about the new crop of young light-heavyweights. He knows how to have a good time. He finds people and places wonderful. "The States were wonderful," he tells Jake. "New York was wonderful." Vienna was wonderful, he writes "Then a card from Budapest: 'Jake, Budapest is wonderful.'" Then he returns to Paris, where Jake greets him:

> "Well," [Jake] said, "I hear you had a wonderful trip."
> "Wonderful," he said. "Budapest is absolutely wonderful."
> "How about Vienna?"
> "Not so good, Jake. Not so good. It seemed better than it was."
> (p. 70)

A few days later, Jake and Bill meet an American family on the train to Pamplona, and the father asks if they're having a good trip. "Wonderful," Bill says (85).

This sort of highly repetitive nonsense is much funnier when spoken than on the page, as Jackson Benson has pointed out.[27] So is the famous stuffed dog discussion on the way to dinner. Jake and Bill walk by a taxidermist's and Bill asks, "Want to buy anything? Nice stuffed dog?"

> "Come on," I said. "You're pie-eyed."
> "Pretty nice stuffed dogs," Bill said. "Certainly brighten up your flat."
> "Come on."
> "Just one stuffed dog. I can take 'em or leave 'em alone. But listen, Jake. Just one stuffed dog."
> "Come on."
> "Mean everything in the world after you bought it. Simple exchange of values. You give them money. They give you a stuffed dog."
> "We'll get one on the way back."

> "All right. Have it your own way. Road to hell paved with un-
> bought stuffed dogs. Not my fault."
> We went on.
> "How'd you feel that way about dogs so sudden?"
> "Always felt that way about dogs. Always been a great lover of
> stuffed animals." (pp. 72–3)

Then they are off on the subject of not being daunted, but Bill understands the humorous potential of the echo. "See that horse-cab?" he asks Jake. "Going to have that horse-cab stuffed for you for Christmas. Going to give all my friends stuffed animals." Brett comes along in a taxi ("'Beautiful lady,'" said Bill. "Going to kidnap us" [74]), and they hit it off beautifully. It is too bad, Bill thinks, that she's engaged to Michael. Still: "What'll I send them? Think they'd like a couple of stuffed race-horses?" (76).

Liquor obviously plays an important role in Bill's comedy. "Don [crossed out] Bill was the best of the lot," Hemingway wrote in a discarded first draft, "and he was on a hilarious drunk and thought everybody else was and became angry if they were not."[28] Alcohol not only fuels his tomfoolery, it also provides him with a potent source of the topical humor that runs through Chapter XII. "Direct action . . . beats legislation," Bill remarks when Jake doctors their rum punches at the inn in Pamplona (123). Bill's voice so predominates in this Burguete section that in the first draft Hemingway tried switching to him as the first-person narrator.[29] Later he went back to Jake as narrator and straight man for Bill's repartee. Among other things, Bill makes fun of the clichés of literary criticism, Bible Belt morality, H. L. Mencken, and – especially – the Scopes trial and William Jennings Bryan's rhetoric in attacking the theory of evolution. Putting aside a hard-boiled egg and unwrapping a drumstick, Bill reverses the order "For Bryan's sake. As a tribute to the Great Commoner. First the chicken; then the egg."

> "Wonder what day God created the chicken?"
> "Oh," said Bill . . . , "how should we know? We should not
> question. Our stay on earth is not for long. Let us rejoice and believe
> and give thanks."

"Let us not doubt, brother," he adds. "Let us not pry into the holy mysteries of the hen-coop with simian fingers." Instead, "Let us utilize the fowls of the air. Let us utilize the product of the vine. Will you utilize a little, brother?'' (121–2). Jake will, and so will Bill, and so will the genial Englishman named Wilson-Harris they play three-handed bridge with in the evening.

As almost every commentator on the novel has noticed, the interlude at Burguete stands in idyllic counterpoint to the sophisticated pretentiousness of Paris and the destructive passions of Pamplona. In the first draft, Hemingway let Jake and Bill confess how they felt about their lives on that fishing trip. No one can believe that he's happy, Bill remarks, but "honest to God," he is. So is Jake, he admits, "ninety percent of the time," although they're both a little embarrassed to confess it.[30] Geography has little to do with this. After their dinner at Madame Lecomte's and a long walk back to Montparnasse, Bill feels so good that he doesn't need a drink. In fact, Jake and Bill are almost always in good spirits when together, either alone or with other male companions. Don Stewart himself blamed the trouble at Pamplona in 1925 on that old "devil sex." The previous year, when he, Ernest, Hadley, John Dos Passos, Bill Bird, and Bob McAlmon had gone to Pamplona for the bullfights, the trip had been a great success.

The Sun Also Rises is the great book it is partly because of Bill Gorton's humor that directs its jibes at ideas and institutions, not human beings. In this way, Gorton provides a model of behavior that – unlike the code of the intrepid Romero – it is possible to emulate. "I did not care that it was all about," Jake reflects in one of his interior monologues. "All I wanted to know was how to live in it" (148). Gorton seems to have discovered how: without Jake's bitter sarcasm, without Mike's and Brett's disingenuous self-depreciation, without Robert's self-pity, with the best will in the world.

Not everyone, it might be objected, is temperamentally suited to enjoy life as much as Gorton, just as very few could be expected to entertain one's companions as well as he. Yet in the very subject matter of his humor, Hemingway conveys an attitude toward existence available to all. It is easiest to understand, through negation, which attitudes are invalid. The religious preach brotherhood and arrange for special privileges. The do-gooding of the Prohibitionists does no good. The know-nothingism of what are currently called "creationists" is ridiculous, and so is the catchword pedantry of the literati: "Irony and Pity." More positively, at least one basic value emerges in the subtext of such ventures into comedy as the twelve shoeshines Bill buys Mike Campbell and his persistent sales pitch for stuffed dogs.

The shoeshine scene represents Bill's humor for once gone off the rails under the tensions of Pamplona. When bootblack after bootblack polishes Mike's shoes to a higher gloss, the repetition becomes more awkward than amusing. As Mike sardonically observes, "Bill's a yell of laughter" (173). By contrast, not even a taxidermist would be likely to find the stuffed dog passage unfunny. Whether successful in inducing laughter or not, however, both scenes have a bearing on the theme of compensation in the novel.[31] Rather casually dropped into the stuffed dog dialogue is Bill's comment about "Simple exchange of values. You give them money. They give you a stuffed dog." This seemingly innocent observation underscores Hemingway's theme that the good things in life — not exclusively limited to hedonistic pleasure — have to be earned through effort and experience. It is for this reason, in part, that the shoeshine episode falls flat, since Bill's jesting contradicts that message by demeaning the low but honest trade of the bootblacks.

In his autobiography, Donald Ogden Stewart chastised himself for having produced so much of the "crazy humor" characteristic of Bill Gorton and pervasive in such Stewart books of the period as *A Parody Outline of History* (1921), *Perfect Behavior*, a 1922 takeoff on Emily Post, *Aunt Polly's Story of Mankind* (1923), *Mr. and Mrs. Haddock Abroad* (1924), *The Crazy Fool* (1925), and *Mr. and Mrs. Haddock in Paris, France* (1926). As his political beliefs swung to the left, Stewart came to believe that he should have used his gift for humor less to amuse his readers than to alert them to the ills of American society. And he seems never to have recognized the accomplishment of his friend Hemingway, whom he thought an indifferent humorist, in incorporating certain strains of humor, including his own nonsensical and topical predilections, within the framework of a novel that has an ethical, if not a political, statement to make.

Hemingway's early humor consisted mostly of parodies and

pieces that mocked others and tacitly asserted his superiority. Later in his career his humor became increasingly dark, as in the macabre "A Natural History of the Dead" (1932). In the course of writing an unpublished tale along similar grisly lines, Hemingway took issue with the claim of Henry Seidel Canby that there was "no humor in American writing . . . no humor in the way we write nor in the things we write about. I always thought there was but perhaps it was not clear enough; it needed a label so that they [the critics] would know it was funny when they read it."[32] *The Sun Also Rises* does not carry such a label, nor does it need to. In this novel alone, Hemingway used humor brilliantly to assess character and underline theme without descending to parody or black comedy. *The Sun Also Rises* stands as proof that Hemingway was "above all a magnificent craftsman, and among his prime virtues was the ability to laugh."[33]

NOTES

1. Charles A. Fenton, *The Apprenticeship of Ernest Hemingway: The Early Years* (New York: Viking, 1958), p. 12.
2. Ernest Hemingway, "Ring Lardner, Jr., Discourses on Editorials," Oak Park *Trapeze* 16 (February 1917):3.
3. Ernest Hemingway, "Dedicated to F.W.," Oak Park *Trapeze* 24 (November 1916):4.
4. The plot of "A Matter of Colour" is summarized in Carlos Baker, *Ernest Hemingway: A Life Story* (New York: Scribners, 1969), pp. 22–3.
5. Donald M. Wright, "A Mid-Western Ad Man Remembers," *Advertising & Selling* 28 (March 25, 1937):54.
6. "The Battle of Copenhagen" is reprinted in *Ernest Hemingway: 88 Poems,* ed. Nicholas Gerogiannis (New York: Harcourt Brace Jovanovich/Bruccoli Clark, 1979), pp. 22–4.
7. Quoted in Fenton, *Apprenticeship,* p. 72.
8. Delmore Schwartz, "The Fiction of Ernest Hemingway," *Perspectives U.S.A.* no. 13 (Autumn 1955):71.
9. "Our Confidential Vacation Guide" appears in *Hemingway: The Wild Years,* ed. Gene Z. Hanrahan (New York: Dell, 1962), pp. 38–41.
10. "Condensing the Classics," Toronto *Star Weekly,* August 20, 1921, p. 22, quoted in Robert O. Stephens, *Hemingway's Nonfiction: The Public*

Voice (Chapel Hill: University of North Carolina Press, 1968), pp. 110–11.

11. Ernest Hemingway, "A Divine Gesture," *Double Dealer* 3 (May 1922): 267–8.

12. Fenton, *Apprenticeship*, p. 260.

13. Ernest Hemingway, *The Torrents of Spring* (New York: Scribners, 1926), pp. 32, 35–6, 42. Thomas N. Hagood draws attention to this pattern in "Elements of Humor in Ernest Hemingway," his 1968 Ph.D. dissertation at Louisiana State University.

14. A. E. Hotchner, *Papa Hemingway* (New York: Random House, 1966), p. 70.

15. Epigraph to *Torrents*, p. 16.

16. See Lloyd Frankenburg, "Themes and Characters in Hemingway's Latest Period," *Southern Review* 7 (Spring 1942):787–8.

17. Ernest Hemingway, *A Moveable Feast* (New York: Scribners, 1964), pp. 29–31.

18. Ernest Hemingway, Item 202c, Hemingway Archive, Kennedy Library, Boston. I am indebted to Michael S. Reynolds for letting me consult his notes on this manuscript.

19. Paul Morreall, *Taking Laughter Seriously* (Albany: State University of New York Press, 1983). The section on incongruity of presentation is on pp. 69–84.

20. Sheldon Norman Grebstein, *Hemingway's Craft* (Carbondale: Southern Illinois University, 1973), p. 172. Grebstein's chapter on Hemingway's humor remains the best discussion of the subject.

21. James Hinkle, "What's Funny in *The Sun Also Rises*," *Proceedings of the First National Conference of the Hemingway Society*, Traverse City, Michigan, October 20–3, 1983, pp. 62–71.

22. The alternative endings are cited in Baker, *Hemingway*, p. 155.

23. In his first draft, Hemingway explicitly associates the women in this coterie with sexual adventurism involving handsome young men like Romero. Item 202c, Hemingway Archive, Kennedy Library, Boston.

24. Morreall, *Taking Laughter Seriously*, pp. 112–13.

25. See Stewart's autobiography, *By a Stroke of Luck* (London: Paddington Press, 1975).

26. F. Scott Fitzgerald, "Reminiscences of Donald Stewart," St. Paul *Daily News*, December 11, 1921, City Life section, p. 6, in *F. Scott Fitzgerald in His Own Time: A Miscellany*, ed. Matthew J. Bruccoli and Jackson R. Bryer (Kent, Ohio: Kent State University Press, 1971), pp. 231–2.

27. Jackson J. Benson, *Hemingway: The Writer's Art of Self-Defense* (Minneapolis: University of Minnesota Press, 1969), pp. 68–9.

28. Item 202c, Hemingway Archive, Kennedy Library, Boston.
29. This experiment in shifting points of view was noted by Frederic Joseph Svoboda, *Hemingway and The Sun Also Rises: The Crafting of a Style* (Lawrence: University Press of Kansas, 1983), p. 42.
30. Item 202c, Hemingway Archive, Kennedy Library, Boston.
31. For a fuller discussion of this theme, see Scott Donaldson, "The Morality of Compensation," in *By Force of Will: The Life and Art of Ernest Hemingway* (New York: Viking, 1977), pp. 21–33.
32. Item 636, Hemingway Archive, Kennedy Library, Boston.
33. Grebstein, *Hemingway's Craft,* p. 201.

The *Sun* in Its Time: Recovering the Historical Context

MICHAEL S. REYNOLDS

MORE than a half century has now passed since we saw the first light of Hemingway's *The Sun Also Rises* – a half century of bloody war and remarkable change: the jet age, the atomic age, the computer age. Next summer at Pamplona the grandchildren of the twenties will make the pilgrimage, looking under the Irunia arcade for an experience trapped in time. In Paris they will sip their beers under the red and gold awnings of the Dome, imagining faces long since gone under the earth. Great books have a way of doing that to us, a way of stopping time. Nostalgia is infectious and easily forgiven. But critics should know better. The places and the weather may look the same, but all else has changed. The music has changed. The clothes have changed. The prices, the moods, the politics, the values – all irrevocably changed. Brett Ashley and Jake Barnes are no longer our contemporaries. Hemingway, as he said of Henry James, is as dead as he will ever be; to continue to read his first novel as if it were written for our age is to be hopelessly romantic.

The Sun's timeless quality, of course, encourages such behavior, but to persist at it past the point of diminished returns is to devalue the novel. *The Sun Also Rises* is a period piece, a historical artifact as precisely dated as that frozen moment at Pompeii. The year is 1925 as it was in another country. The book could not have been written any earlier, for the Great War had not yet produced the war-wounded generation that peoples *The Sun*. A decade later it would not have been written; in the middle of the Great Depression, no one was interested in boozy expatriates. We can no more properly read *The Sun Also Rises* outside of its social and historical context than we can view Picasso's "Les Demoiselles d'Avignon" as if it

43

were painted last year. Both are works of art anchored in time. To treat either artist as if he were our contemporary is to pretend that we are living in an earlier age. Foolishness, utterly. Our time is not their time. Historically blind readers see only the timeless qualities of the work, and even those they are reading at a discount.

Unfortunately, Hemingway's roman à clef has suffered from one kind of historical context that has severely blurred the novel's true focus. Basing several of the characters, as he did, on real people, Hemingway encouraged readers and critics to waste inordinate effort documenting the parallels. While Hemingway was revising his first draft of *The Sun,* he told Ernest Walsh:

> I believe that when you are writing stories about actual people, not the best thing to do, you should make them those people in every-thing except telephone addresses. Think that is the only justification for writing stories about actual people.[1]

Some of the earliest reviewers, wanting to dismiss *The Sun* as a trashy novel, picked on this element. The *New York World* said:

> For those who know the stamping ground of the American expatri-ates in Paris – that district clustered about the corner where the Boulevard Raspail crosses the Boulevard Montparnasse – it will become speedily patent that practially all of these characters are directly based on actual people.[2]

The biographical reading of the novel continued until the real characters – Duff Twysden, Pat Guthrie, Harold Loeb, Niño de la Palma – became as familiar as their fictional avatars – Brett, Mike, Cohn, and Pedro Romero. Today the prototypes are all dead, and the reader no longer cares if Duff went to San Sabastian with Loeb or slept with Niño. There remains, however, the tendency to see Jake Barnes as a thinly veiled version of Hemingway himself. To take two steps into that literary bog is to become mired in fictional biography, which is not only factually false but which also says precious little about the novel itself.

Each generation, of course, will read *The Sun* through its own prevailing filter, finding there its own needs. The beat generation of the fifties thought the Paris-Pamplona lifestyle admirable, an early version of *On the Road.* The romantic revolutionaries in the sixties related to Hemingway's war-wounded band of revelers as fellow travelers rejecting the false values of a corrupt society. The conservatives of the eighties, on the other hand, find little to admire in the novel. They condone neither Brett's promiscuity nor Cohn's hopeless romantic ideals. For this present generation, *The Sun Also Rises* is a study in moral failure, a jaded world of unemployed and irresponsible characters who drink too much — a fable of ideological bankruptcy. Ironically, this present age is closer to Hemingway's original view than most of us realize.

As he finished the manuscript in 1926, Hemingway joked with Scott Fitzgerald that he would dedicate the book:

TO MY SON
John Hadley Nicanor
This Collection of Instructive Anecdotes[3]

Fitzgerald, who took him seriously, urged Hemingway to rethink the dedication. Hemingway replied, "It is so obviously *not* a collection of instructive anecdotes and is such a hell of a sad story — and not one at all for a child to read — and the only instruction is how people go to hell . . . that I thought it pleasant to dedicate it to Bumby."[4]

Most of his readers that year missed the point. Too deeply involved, perhaps, in the conflicting lifestyles of Prohibition, they either condemned the book and its author without understanding the ironic message or longed to drink at the same Paris bars. Hemingway complained to his editor, "It's funny to write a book that seems as tragic as that and have them take it for a jazz superficial story."[5] *Such a hell of a sad story . . . tragic . . . how people go to hell:* Perhaps we have been missing the point. Perhaps Hemingway was more of a moralist than is commonly granted him. Echoing James's Winterborne, Hemingway in 1926 felt out of touch with the American reader: "In several ways I have been long enough in Europe."[6]

Hemingway had not lost touch; he had touched too hard. He had his fingers too firmly on the moral pulse of his times for most American readers to appreciate his moral indictment. In his unpublished forward to *The Sun Also Rises*, Hemingway said:

> This is not a question of what kind of mothers will flappers make or where is bobbed hair leading us. This is about something that is

45

already finished. For whatever is going to happen to the generation of which I am a part has already happened.[7]

It was more than the Great War that had "already happened." The war merely put a period on the end of a sentence that had been twenty years in the writing. The stable values of 1900 had eroded beneath the feet of this generation: Home, family, church, and country no longer gave the moral support that Hemingway's generation grew up with. The old values — honor, duty, love — no longer rang as true as they had in the age of Teddy Roosevelt. For Hemingway and for the country, the loss was not permanent, but in 1926 it seemed that it was. If his characters seemed degenerate, if their values appeared shallow, so did the world appear, at home and abroad, in those postwar years. To read Hemingway's indictment of his age as a paean to the "lost generation" is to miss his point badly.

As with so many of the modernists, Hemingway's modernism resided in his style, not in his ideas or his value system. He was not as politically conservative as Yeats, and in later years he claimed to be apolitical or an anarchist, in favor of as little government as possible. However, growing up in Oak Park's conservative Republican bastion where his grandfather never sat knowingly at the same table with a Democrat, Hemingway retained many of the stalwart ideals embodied by Theodore Roosevelt. As Roosevelt advocated the moral and physical "strenuous life," so did Hemingway. Hard work was always his cardinal virtue. In his letters he continually assured recipients that he was working diligently. In *The Sun,* work separates the amateurs from the professionals. Pedro Romero is a professional, who performs at the height of his talent no matter what the circumstances. We admire that in Romero because Jake Barnes admires it. Ironically, Georgette, the prostitute, is also a professional. She works her trade of whoring without compromising her standards. Compared with Brett Ashley, Georgette is virtuous: Georgette whores from economic need; Brett whores from psychic need. Neither Jake nor the reader quite forgives her for her liaison with Cohn.

On the surface, it would appear that Hemingway is satirizing the work ethic through Jake's ironic commentary on "the clear financial basis" of relationships, but the reader must remember that we are listening to a narrator whose traditional values are no longer current. The voice, detached and understated, is filled with irony and not a little bitterness. If professional employment no longer matters in his age, it is not his fault, nor does he approve of the loss. Jake Barnes is a newspaperman, who writes his copy, sends his wires, and saves his money for the festival at Pamplona. The others — like the "rotten crowd" of *The Great Gatsby* — do not work. Cohn gets support checks from his mother; Mike Campbell, a bankrupt, gets a family allowance; Brett Ashley lives precariously on support money from her second husband. "You have nice friends," Georgette tells Jake. In Pamplona, the hotel owner, Montoya, will forgive many failings in a man with *afición*. Jake tells us, "At once he forgave me all my friends. Without his ever saying anything they were simply a little something shameful between us" (132).

Money, as more than one critic has told us, becomes a satiric device in the novel, due largely to Jake's continuous references to paying bills. "The bill," he tells us, "always came. That was one of the swell things you could count on" (148). It is Jake who pays the bills — bar bills, hotel bills, and bills of moral debt. In the end, as we will see, the bill for Pamplona is far greater than he expected. But Jake does not equate the value of work with money. It is the world in which he lives, not Jake Barnes, that has reduced everything to such a "clear financial basis." Jake's insistence on getting good value for money spent, on paying his way in the world, "seemed like a fine philosophy" to him, but it is the philosophy of his times, not one he invented or one of which he approves. "In five years," he tells himself, "it will seem just as silly as all the other fine philosophies I've had" (148). Five years later, in 1931, Jake might have told the country plunging into the Depression: "I told you so."

Wherever Hemingway looked in 1925, he saw dollar signs. Everything was for sale, its price clearly marked. At the postwar conferences — Versailles, Genoa, Lausanne — the future of Europe was on the auction block. At home, sons of bankers married Follies stars who sold their svelte bodies for immediate returns. The Teapot Dome scandal took Harry Sinclair and the Standard Oil

Company to court: A simple exchange of values – Harry had given the secretary of the interior money in exchange for the navy's oil reserves. Meanwhile, the banker Mellon, as secretary of the treasury, was protecting his own companies from paying federal taxes. Easy money. Quick money. Bootlegger money. In 1923 the tax returns showed 74 millionaires, but those were only the ones who declared honest income. The Paris *Tribune* headlines kept the young writer's nose rubbed in the money pot:

U.S. PROSPERITY IS
GREATEST IN HISTORY

Hoover Credits "Era Of Good Times"
To High Wages, Steady Employment.
Wall Street Prices Soar   (November 8, 1925)

The bull market roared and the dollar climbed, peaking that fall at 26 francs when a half franc bought a mug of beer, 1.65 francs bought a loaf of bread, and 800 francs rented a furnished flat for a month. Americans flowed into Paris, changing everything. By early 1924, 100,000 English-speaking residents crowded the city; during the summer season their number doubled. On the Left and Right banks, Americans were everywhere. They could be seen "on any night of July or August packing the Dome or the Dingo or the Select. . . . the most conspicuous one is the flapper who has skipped school and come to see 'life' and the corresponding pink-cheeked, well-scrubbed college boy" (*Tribune*, August 23, 1925). More and more clubs, bars, and dancings opened up to water the crowd, to cater to American money. Prices went up, gentrifying the old bohemian way of life. In the Latin Quarter, fewer and fewer real artists and writers did decent work.

Some of the old hands went back to the States, complaining that "before the old Dome was frequented by a little family of artists, whereas it has now become a sort of open air post-graduate school for tourists to study life" (*Tribune*, August 6, 1925). Others, like Harold Stearns, who appears in *The Sun* as Harvey Stone, tried to go home and found they could not live there either. Stearns wrote:

I had to go back home to discover that I was an American through and through. . . . Also I had to go back home to discover that it would be impossible ever again to live happily in America. . . .

48

Everybody was dissatisfied, everybody was hysterical. . . . in New York nobody was happy, not even when a new case of gin was delivered. Everybody was hectic, making money furiously, working at the game of pretending to work, shameless and audacious in their heterogenerous love-making to a point where I, a quiet and respectable citizen of Paris, was actually embarrassed. . . . With so many churches and religious alarums, I never found fewer people who realized that religion has no civilized appeal above and beyond its purely esthetic one. (*Tribune,* May 3, 1925)

Also American through and through, Jake Barnes cannot go home, for his prewar value system no longer has a home. Like one of Conrad's representative men set down in another country, Jake is the moral barometer of the novel. There is nothing wrong with his values: Work, duty, sympathy, brotherhood, professional pride, and financial responsibility once sustained middle-class America. It is not Jake who fails, but America who fails him.

He lives in a Paris so thoroughly Americanized that it is seldom necessary to speak French. In *The Sun* there are no important French characters; we never see French life. To read the novel, as some did, as an exemplum of foreign degenerate values is to read it blind. As the Paris *Tribune* remarked:

We have American bars in Paris, an American Hospital in Paris, American Jazz-Bands, American Newspapers, American Crooks, Philanthropists, Barbers, Dentists, Doctors, and American Under-takers in Paris. We have an American Library in Paris, an American Legion, a Chamber of Commerce, a Women's Club, a University Union, a Cathedral, several Churches, numerous American Banks to draw our money out of, and plenty of American Habits to spend it on. (May 24, 1925)

The only remaining standard, as Count Mippipopolous knew, was getting good value for one's money. Early in the novel Jake may agree, but after paying so many bills, he finds himself short-changed in Pamplona, where he gets nothing like good value for his money.

Americans who stayed home understood the count perfectly. As the first wave of consumer technology hit the marketplace, Americans were hard put to keep up with the myriad new devices. By 1923, Henry Ford and his peers were parking 4 million new automobiles in front of American homes. Across the country vaudeville theaters were converting to movie houses. Everything was modern; everything was electric: sewing machines, refrigerators, radios, hair dryers, vacuum cleaners, phonographs, toasters. By 1927 half of the American households owned a record player, a car, and a telephone. We had become a nation of consumers, paying for the new technology in installments. Debt became a way of life in the rush to buy now, live now. American readers, who found Hemingway's novel so lacking in positive moral values, were themselves the willing participants in the nation's first great buying binge. If money seems the only significant value in *The Sun Also Rises*, Hemingway did not create that moral climate, nor does Jake Barnes approve of those who live on the financial brink. "The bill always came," he tells us. "That was one of the swell things you could count on."

Hemingway's Oak Park background never allowed him to despise money. He did not subscribe to any romantic notions about the starving artist, not in those days. In his dotage he might say that hunger was good for the writer, but in those early Paris days, when he was never truly poor, he intended to make a decent living from his writing. Money per se was not corrupting so long as one worked for it. The Americans and British in Paris were not working; that was the burr that galled him. The readers offended by *The Sun Also Rises* did not see that Jake Barnes was equally offended. Because of Jake's reticence, we hear only his understated and ironic bitterness. In 1926, three years away from the money bubble's bursting, Hemingway, like Fitzgerald, had his finger on the sick pulse of an era about to fail. *Hold him in your arms and you can feel his disease,* as the children of a later generation chanted.

The novel may not be tragic, but it does capture a time and place, reflecting accurately the failings of an age. At least one reviewer understood that "any country's condition can be deduced from the vices and virtues of the expatriates. In them the native attributes are in excess."[8] Today historians and sociologists frequently quote *The Sun* to emphasize the moral dither of those postwar years. Beneath the humorous banter of Bill Gorton, we catch allusions to the American scene, allusions now largely lost on the reader. Today our concept of the twenties has been too thoroughly clouded by Hollywood images of gangsters, speakeasies, short skirts, blaring jazz, and polished automobiles. We have forgotten how reactionary the period actually was.

As Bill and Jake fish above Burguete, Bill makes anachronistic jokes about the death of William Jennings Bryan, the Great Commoner who had become a right-wing, moral reactionary. In 1925 at the Scopes Monkey Trial in Tennessee, fundamentalist Bryan aided the successful prosecutor in upholding the state's law against the teaching of evolution. In the middle of the 1925 Pamploma festival, the Paris *Tribune* headline read:

> BRYAN OPENS ATTACK
> AT SCOPES TRIAL
>
> Proclaiming "Fight to Death" Against Evolution,
> Silver-Tongued Orator Gets Ovation at Dayton
> (July 9, 1925)

Today we think of the Scopes trial as an anomaly. It was not. What happened in Tennessee was symptomatic of what was happening in the country. After the corrupt Harding administration, the voters put another Republican, Coolidge, in the White House with a larger plurality than any before in American history. In Congress the first Equal Rights Amendment for women failed; they had the vote – enough was enough. In August 1925, those same congressmen watched 100,000 Ku Klux Klansmen parade down Pennsylvania Avenue dressed in white sheets, their hoods hanging down behind them. No need to hide their faces in the American twenties. On some college campuses, the KKK was just another student organization.

In a 1923 article warning against the *potential* crimes of the Ku Klux Klan, the *New Republic* understood perfectly the mood of white America:

> The Ku Klux Klan holds that the dearest values in American life are Protestantism; white supremacy, in America and the world; Anglo-Saxon legal institutions; the system of free private enterprise. . . . These are respectable values.

The menace was clear:

> Jews and Catholics . . . are steadily gaining by natural increase. Both are advancing in economic power, the Jews especially; both are winning political power, especially the Catholics. . . . the yellow

51

race is taking Hawaii and the Negro race does not look forward to an indefinite period of political exclusion in the South. . . . And as for the enemies of free enterprise and private property, their number is certainly considerable. (January 17, 1923, p. 189)

Jake Barnes is not reassured when Bill Gorton tells him that everything is swell in the States. Jake, like his creator Hemingway, reads the magazines and papers.

Those were the years when a nation whose entire population traced its roots to immigrants began to fear foreigners. Burned by Wilson's idealism in the Great War, America burrowed into an isolationist policy and its first red scare. The Bolsheviks, as if they did not have enough problems in Russia, were said to be plotting the overthrow of our way of life. Socialism was just another name for Communism, and labor unions were thought to be its leading advocates. During the twenties, union membership fell by half; political ideas became dangerous. By 1924 in California, ninety-six men were in state prisons, convicted of political beliefs contrary to the majority view. On the heels of the 1919 Palmer Acts, which deported politically undesirable aliens, the U.S. Congress in 1924 passed the National Origins Act, which limited European immigration by a quota system and totally excluded all Asians. The 1925 U.S. Army war games, staged in Hawaii, were an exercise in defending the islands from a hypothetical Japanese invasion. The next war, many were certain, would be fought against the "yellow horde." In Boston, meanwhile, two Italian immigrants – Sacco and Vanzetti, convicted on questionable evidence of a capital crime – were under sentence of death, victims of the times. The ironic phrase "One Hundred Percent American" became part of our lexicon. Bill Gorton tells Jake, "Fake European standards have ruined you" (115). Bill means it as a joke. At home it was no joke. *The American Mercury,* with the emphasis on *American,* satirized the cosmopolitan with his foreign tastes:

The smart American drinks St. Emilion, Graves, St. Julien and Macon, the beverages of French peasants. He plays Mah Jong, the game of Chinese coolies. He wears, on Sundays, a cutaway coat, the garb of English clerks. His melodic taste is for jazz, the music of African niggers. He eats alligator pears, the food of Costa Rican billy goats.[9]

The American scene, of which Hemingway's first readers were a part, was filled with fears and prejudices, all in the name of nationalism.

Not the least of those fears was the virulent strain of anti-Semitism that broke out in America after the Great War. Today we remember Hitler's "final solution" for the Jewish question and are appalled. We have conveniently forgotten auto maker Henry Ford and his Dearborn *Independent,* which spewed out a steady stream of Jew-baiting sewage. We have forgotten the "Protocols of the Elders of Zion," a trumped-up anti-Semitic document purporting to be the Jews' master plan to take over Western civilization. We have forgotten Harvard President Abbott Lawrence Lowell's "solution" to widespread anti-Semitism on the college campuses of the twenties. He said:

> There is most unfortunately a rapidly growing anti-Semitic feeling in this country. The question for those of us who deplore such a state of things is how it can be combatted. If every college in the country would take a limited proportion of Jews, I suspect we should go a long way toward eliminating race feeling among the students.[10]

To read *The Sun Also Rises* right, we must remember something of those times.

The first thing Jake tells us about Cohn is that he is a Jew who went to Princeton, where a boxing match "certainly improved his nose." Cohn, we hear, "was a member, through his father, of one of the richest Jewish families in New York, and through his mother of one of the oldest" (3–4). The American reader in 1926 would have picked up those signals: Cohn belonged to the Jewish establishment, which many thought to be a threat to the American way of life. Jake tries to like Cohn but finds him a boor, just as we do today, for Robert Cohn has plenty of dislikable characteristics without his Jewishness being part of the issue. But it is there. Jake never lets the reader forget it. When Cohn first sees Brett Ashley, Jake says he "looked a great deal as his compatriot must have looked when he first saw the promised land" (22). When Cohn says that Jake is the best friend he has, Jake thinks to himself, "God help you" (39). Jake, badly hurt when Brett takes Cohn with her for a week at San Sebastian, does not resort to Jew baiting, but his friends do. Bill wonders, "Why didn't she go off with some of her own people?" (102). And Mike says, "Brett's gone off with men. But they weren't Jews" (143). Brett's promiscuity they can forgive, but not her choice of a Jew.

Readers today are apt to say that Hemingway's depiction of Robert Cohn betrays his anti-Semitism, which it does — the same anti-Semitism found in T. S. Eliot and Ezra Pound. In the twenties this attitude was so prevalent that it was an unremarkable, almost unconscious response. Jake Barnes, in fact, bends over backward to be nice to Cohn — almost reverse discrimination. At Scribners, Max Perkins would not let Hemingway use the word "balls," but he did not blink at the word "kike." But to fault Hemingway for his prejudice is to read the novel anachronistically. In 1926 none of the reviewers remarked on Hemingway's treatment of Robert Cohn; his behavior was just what they expected from a rich New York Jew who did not know his place. The novel's anti-Semitism tells us little about its author but a good deal about America in 1926. To forget how we were in the twenties is to read the novel out of context.

If we forget, for example, just how schizophrenic American moral behavior became in the twenties, we do not fully understand the same curious moral division in *The Sun*. Henry Adams was barely moldering before his prediction that there would never be an American Venus went as flat as the silver screen on which she appeared. Hollywood gave American girls a new role model — the vamp — whose style infected shop girls in Des Moines and kid sisters in Topeka. Corsets disappeared, skirts flapped above the knees, stockings rolled, and one-piece bathing suits clung revealingly to America's daring daughters. The first generation to learn about sexual relationships from the movies began to alienate their parents. When their children embraced Negro jazz music, the parents, for whom the foxtrot was daring and the tango salacious, despaired.

Violent action, in moral Newtonian terms, produced a violent reaction. The Seventh Day Adventists predicted the imminent end of the world; the beast of the apocalypse was upon them. Fundamentalist religions moaned and multiplied; Billy Sunday, sliding in the aisles, led the moral revival with typical American show-manship. Cardinal Hayes pleaded with America to return to God:

> The claim of a new personal freedom — to do as one wants, unrestrained by standards of right and wrong — cannot fail to produce an unhealthy reaction in society. . . . Naked, brutish realism, with a boldness hitherto unknown, challenges from the very housetops, and the distinction of what is clean or unclean, healthy or putrid in literature, art, drama, and public exhibitions is fast being lost sight of. (*Tribune*, January 5, 1925)

While its younger generation went temporarily crazy, the American moral majority frantically tightened the loose screws of the moral locks. Joyce's *Ulysses* was banned from import just when the new American writers most needed it. Local governments created a plethora of censorship laws to keep virginal minds pure. Publishers walked in fear of censorship. Scribners would not let Mike Campbell say "The bulls have no balls," for they were sure that word alone would doom the book. Under pressure, Hemingway changed it to "The bulls have no horns." In the *Tribune*, Mencken fumed about the Clean Books Bill. "The aim of this bill," he said, "is to make it impossible for a publisher accused of publishing an immoral book to make any defense at all" (January 11, 1925).

Not even Paris, which home-bound Americans knew to be Sin City, was exempt from the reformers, who exported their zeal, along with the Rotary Club, to France. They tried in 1925 to clean up the nightclub acts, which were filled with American show girls playing mostly to tourist audiences. They failed. On January 8, 1925, "The pretty Hoffman girls performing 'Black Mass' in Montmartre were cleared of charges of indecency filed by 'reformers'" (*Tribune*). That was the year that Harry Pilcer put bare-breasted feather dancers into his Acacia Club and Josephine Baker, black, beautiful, and very bare, lit up the Paris night in the Revue Negre. Parisians might not approve of all that jazz, but they were not going to let American prudery dictate their entertainment any more than they were going to allow the Prohibition movement to gain a foothold in Gaul.

Prohibition, of course, was the most obvious example of the insane division in the American moral fabric. By 1925 the *New*

Republic, the *American Mercury,* and most of the newspapers were reporting a continuing dialogue between those who were certain that Prohibition was a ridiculous failure and their moral opponents who argued that it was working. That spring the U.S. Navy and Coast Guard sent out an armed flotilla to prevent organized rum runners from landing on the East Coast. The results were as mixed as the cocktails that half of America consumed and that the *Mercury* called an American art form. In Congress, the drinkers kept trying to take the edge off Prohibition without alienating the voters back home. Moral opponents turned back their every effort.

As Bill and Jake "utilize" their wine, they joke about Wayne B. Wheeler and the Anti-Saloon League. Wheeler was no joke, as the *Tribune's* editorial shows:

> Wayne B. Wheeler, who keeps Congress in line for the Anti-Saloon League, says that the fifty congressmen who are for the 2.75 beer are bung-starters and they had better make their stuff good by doing it April 1. He says Congress cannot legalize 2.75 beer because it is intoxicating, and the Constitution prohibits intoxicating beverages.
>
> Mr. Wheeler should put his shirt back on. Congress will not hurt the Constitution by redefining intoxicating beverages. . . . Wheeler says that patriotic ex-service men resent the effort to make them stand for beer by saying that the tax on it would pay their bonus. He is convinced that the soldiers will give up their bonus rather than take beer along with it. Maybe so, but it may be news to a great many men who fought in France. (March 24, 1924)

The bill failed. Americans did not get their beer; the vets did not get their bonus, and the money kept rolling into the speakeasies. By the time Prohibition fell of its own weight in the thirties, it was uncertain which had cost the government more: the price of ineffectually enforcing the law or the taxes lost in illegal consumption.

If the sundowners in Hemingway's novel seem today to drink excessively, we must remember the backdrop against which they were drinking. Jake has lived long enough in foreign parts to drink without making it a political statement. In Paris, he is never drunk. On the other hand, Bill Gorton, who is visiting from the States, seems continually tipsy – the American abroad who has to catch up. On the train to Bayonne, Jake and Bill meet a more representative American couple who appreciate a drink now and then. The wife says, "I voted against prohibition to please him, and because I like a little beer in the house" (86). At Burguete, Bill and Jake get a bit potted on just two bottles of wine, but it is not until the festival begins that Jake's heavy drinking starts. No one there thinks Jake's inebriation remarkable, for San Fermin is powered by alcohol. Next summer in Pamplona, the moderate American drinker will still be surprised by the flowing wine. Before the festival is finished, he will have either joined the crowd or not enjoyed the experience. Jake's drinking, however, is an escape mechanism that he uses to avoid thinking about his condition or the disaster taking place around him. In Madrid, when he no longer has the excuse of the festival, Jake gets bloody drunk while Brett tells him that there is no need for it. But there is a need, for Jake knows too well his bankrupt condition. Flat broke in spirit, he can face no more moral bills. To appreciate fully the vintage bouquet of *The Sun,* the reader needs both text and subtext.

To forget the subtext is also to miss a good deal of Hemingway's wit and irony. For example, when Jake and Bill travel to Bayonne, the train is jammed with American pilgrims on their way to Lourdes. The "mackerel snappers" Bill calls them, referring to the Catholic practice of eating fish on Friday. When he and Jake cannot get a seating in the dining car, Bill jokingly says, "It's enough to make a man join the Klan." In those days in America the KKK and other hate groups feared the Catholics even more than they feared the Jews. Publications like *The Menace* kept 100 percent Americans informed of the popish threat to our sovereignty. But underneath Bill Gorton's banter lies a more subtle joke that a 1926 reader would have caught.

Lourdes, where the Virgin Mary appeared to a peasant girl — Marie Bernadette — was already a holy site where the lame and the sick sought miraculous cures. In the summer of 1925 the Lourdes mania reached an almost hysterical pitch when on June 14 the pope canonized Sister Marie Bernadette a saint of the Catholic Church. All that summer the southbound trains were jammed with pilgrims. On August 22, 1925, just as Hemingway arrived back in Paris with his first draft of *The Sun* almost complete, the *Tribune's* front page told him:

PILGRIMAGE TO LOURDES STARTS

The world-famous Pyreneean pilgrimage town is in high excitement . . . nineteen special trains from all parts of France are con-
veying the faithful to Lourdes to celebrate the fifty-third French
National pilgrimage to the shrine of Notre-Dame de Lourdes.

On September 8, the Feast of the Nativity of the Blessed Virgin,
60,000 pilgrims set a one-day record at Lourdes. When Jake
Barnes crosses the path of the Catholics bound for Lourdes, Hemingway's irony redoubles. If ever a man needed a miraculous cure,
it is Jake Barnes. He, too, is on a pilgrimage to the annual feast of
San Fermin and the pagan fertility ritual of the bull ring. As a
nominally practicing Catholic, Jake is making the wrong pilgrimage. To miss the references is to miss the point.

Our time is not the *The Sun's* time. Today Brett Ashley, with her
liberated attitudes, seems our contemporary; in the twenties she
was not the norm, but the new wave. In 1925 she was on the
leading edge of the sexual revolution that produced two types of
the "new woman": the educated professional woman who was
active in formerly all-male areas and the stylish, uninhibited
young woman who drank and smoked in public, devalued sexual
innocence, married but did not want children, and considered
divorce no social stigma. The first type met with sometimes hysterical resistance from male America. Emma Goldman, radical political activist, was deported. Ma Ferguson, elected governor of
Texas, faced rabid male chauvinism in the national press. The
American Mercury, so critical of the country's cultural wasteland,
still felt that woman's place was in the home:

As soon as a woman steps into the male motley, her dignity begins
to vanish. . . . She idiotically assumes that a day of feminism has
arrived – that it is time to cast off certain "shackles" and take her
place beside man, the heroic. . . . Well, it simply won't work.[11]

The so-called ladies' magazines did little to promote economic or
political independence for women. Edited by men, they continued
to portray women in ads, features, and fiction as nest builders. The
movies, on the other hand, turned women into sexual objects,
churning out films like *The Hell Cat, The She Devil, The Scarlet
Woman, The Sin Woman, The Scarlet Sin, The Mortal Sin,* and *Sins of*

58

Mothers. The American male in the twenties could accept woman as either mother or vamp, but not as his economic equal.

Quite obviously Brett Ashley is not a new woman competing in the male marketplace. She is, rather, Hemingway's sophisticated version of the screen vamp. The scene in Pamplona when, wreathed with garlic in the cellar bar, she is surrounded by male dancers could have come from a number of Hollywood films. Twice divorced, Brett has a child she seldom sees; engaged to Mike Campbell, she has seemingly inconsequential affairs with Cohn and Romero that leave her without feelings of guilt or remorse. Brett's rather blasé attitude toward divorce seems today thoroughly modern. In 1926 it was a sign of the times. In 1923 the U.S. divorce rate soared; 165,226 American couples split up that year. For the next several years the figure continued to climb.

The "quickie" divorce was all the rage, and Paris was its center: the divorce mill of Europe. Sparrow Robertson's ad in the Paris *Tribune* was symptomatic of the era: "My wife having left my bed and board I will not be responsible for any bills run up at Kileys, 25 Rue Fontaine, Montmartre" (January 1, 1925). Perhaps because it was more newsworthy, the newspaper emphasized the women who were divorcing their husbands. In 1925, scarcely a week went by without a front-page *Tribune* story of American women granted a Paris divorce.

GLORIA SWANSON GETS PARIS DIVORCE   (Jan. 9)

FOUR AMERICAN WOMEN IN PARIS GET DIVORCES (Apr. 24)

MAE MURRY, FILM STAR, IS DIVORCED   (May 27)

Only the rich or famous made the paper. Hundreds of other American women divorced that year in Paris without much fanfare.

In 1927 Hemingway's marriage to Hadley Richardson became one more number in the growing divorce figure. Although Hemingway himself would divorce three wives, he never did it with ease, always forcing his wife to make the decision. His Oak Park values never allowed him to divorce lightly or without remorse, particularly remorse for leaving Hadley. One subtext for *The Sun Also Rises* is the Hemingway marriage, which was coming apart as Hemingway revised his manuscript. He dedicated the novel to

Hadley and their son, John; in the divorce settlement, he gave Hadley all of the royalties from *The Sun*. Jake is not Hemingway, but Jake's frustration does epitomize that of his author. Raised in a time when sexual continence, fidelity, and the marriage vows were socially binding, Hemingway found himself in a sexually liberated era that he could not participate in without feeling guilty. The nation's sexual dilemma, which Hemingway understood in his private life, finds its ironic metaphor in Jake Barnes. If ever a man was strapped into a moral straightjacket, it is Jake: impotent and impossibly in love with Brett.

Reticent and self-effacing, Jake Barnes is no hero and certainly not a role model for the very young. As the narrator of his own small catastrophe, Jake quietly tries to maintain a little dignity as he presents his case in the court of moral bankruptcy. But even a little dignity is denied him. Bitterly he sums up his case for us: "Send a girl off with a man. Introduce her to another to go off with him. Now go and bring her back. And sign the wire with love. That was it all right" (239). Having pimped away the last vestige of his dignity in Pamplona, he runs to Madrid as soon as he gets the wire: "AM RATHER IN TROUBLE BRETT." Paying the final bill, as it were, Jake spends himself dangerously close to the edge. The only value left in his moral savings account is his work – writing – which he tries to maintain by putting his story on paper.

One recalls the joking charge that Bill made at Burguete:

> "You're an expatriate. You've lost touch with the soil. You get precious. Fake European standards have ruined you. You drink yourself to death. You become obsessed by sex. You spend all your time talking, not working. You are an expatriate, see? You hang around cafes." (p. 115)

He may drink too much and be obsessed by sex, but because Jake works, he never thinks of himself as an expatriate. In the opening chapter of *The Sun*, which got as far as page proof before Hemingway cut it, Jake insisted that the reader understand that he was not one of those who wasted their lives in the cafes:

> I never hung about the Quarter much in Paris until Brett and Mike showed up. I always felt about the Quarter that I could sort of take it or leave it alone. . . . The Quarter is sort of more a state of mind than a geographical area. . . . This state of mind is principally con-

60

tempt. Those who work have the greatest contempt for those who
don't. The loafers are leading their own lives and it is bad form to
mention work.[12]

Jake nevertheless does live in the Latin Quarter, frequenting the
same bars that young Hemingway, barely two months in Paris,
had found so filled with degenerates.

Early in 1922, Hemingway described the Latin Quarter through
the eyes of one deeply shocked by a lifestyle that apparently belit-
tled hard work:

> The scum of Greenwich Village, New York, has been skimmed off
> and deposited in large ladelsful on that section of Paris adjacent to
> the Cafe Rotonde. The new scum, of course, has risen to take the
> place of the old, but the oldest scum, the thickest scum and the
> scummiest scum has come across the ocean, somehow, and with its
> afternoon and evening levees has made the Rotonde the leading
> Latin Quarter show place for tourists in search of atmosphere. . . .
> You can find anything you are looking for at the Rotonde — except
> serious artists . . . for the artists of Paris who are turning out cred-
> itable work resent and loathe the Rotonde crowd . . . [who] are
> nearly all loafers expending the energy that an artist puts into his
> creative work in talking about what they are going to do and con-
> demning the work of all artists who have gained any degree of
> recognition.[13]

For Hemingway and his narrator Jake, work was the litmus test for
distinguishing the man of character from the poseur. Without his
work, Jake Barnes is no better than the rest of the cafe crowd.
Jake's novel — *The Sun Also Rises* — is an act of redemption written
by a troubled man struggling to maintain some sense of dignity.

By 1925, Americans in Paris had become defensive about living
in the Latin Quarter. Like the Haight-Ashbury residents of a later
generation, their address had become tainted in the American
press, and the epithet "expatriate" was onerous. Like Jake, one
letterwriter to the Paris *Tribune* resented the label:

> Men fresh from America . . . go too far when they speak of Ameri-
> cans living in Europe as "expatriates." The word can be twisted by a
> "hundred per-cent American" to mean anything, but obviously it
> means one who has changed his allegiance. . . . France harbors few
> Yankees who are other than Americans. . . . The type of American

that is drawn to France is not of the class that violates laws at home.
(February 15, 1925)

That April in the *Tribune*, H. L. Mencken, while praising writers
who stayed on their native soil, condemned the expatriates whole-
sale: "Artists, indeed, usually suffer damage when they are trans-
planted. The emigrés who flock to Paris, seeking to escape the
horrors of the Puritan *kultur*, find only impotence and oblivion
there; not one of them has written a line worth reading" (April 19,
1925). In September 1925, Mencken followed up with Sinclair
Lewis's broadside blasting the Left Bank loafers. Harold Stearns,
resident intellectual at the Dome and Select, responded in the *Tribune* with biting invective but little substance – an old dog gone in
the teeth.

All that year, while Hemingway was writing his novel about the
Latin Quarter crowd, the battle raged in the *Tribune* and in the
magazines. At year's end, Bruce Bliven, an American political
writer and critic, got in the last word:

> Of course, . . . it may well be the case that of ten Latin Quarter
> aesthetes, one genuine artist may be produced. It may also be true
> that this one artist has a real need for the sort of life the left bank
> offers. In that case, the nine who provide the milieu may well be
> excused for the sake of the tenth. . . . Any writer who is ruined
> even by the Latin Quarter probably would be ruined inevitably, and
> it might as well be the Quarter as anything else. If a man has real
> genius in him and is of a certain temperament, not that of Lewis, the
> Latin Quarter may help him to express himself. On the other hand,
> a good man probably runs little danger of corruption. He will see
> through the foolish aspects of Latin Quarter life soon enough, and
> continue to attend to his work. (*Tribune*, December 2, 1925)

Jake Barnes, who sees through the foolish aspects clearly enough,
appears to himself, by the novel's end, just as foolish as the Latin
Quarter crowd he despises.

In late July 1925, as he and Hadley followed the bullfights south
through Spain, Ernest Hemingway began writing *The Sun Also
Rises*. At Pamplona, the excitement of Niño de la Palma, a promising young matador, captured Hemingway's imagination, but further into the season he watched Niño's skills deteriorate under the

pressures of the professional circuit. When Hemingway began his first draft, he intended to write a novel about a young matador corrupted by the drinking and promiscuity of the Latin Quarter crowd who followed the summer circuit.[14] Begun on the first day of the fiesta, the novel, after establishing the characters and Niño's promise, flashed back to the Latin Quarter so that the reader might understand exactly the sort of people surrounding Niño. Hemingway wrote:

> So I will not judge the gang who were at Pamplona and I will not say that it would be better for Niño de la Palma to be in his grave than to train with a crowd like that because if he did train with them he would be in his grave soon enough and no matter how attractive a grave may seem to old people or to heroes or as an alternative to sin to religious mothers it is no place for a nineteen year old kid.[15]

With the novel barely started, Hemingway reversed his field, fictionalized the names of his characters, created Jake Barnes as the narrator, and began again. He must have realized that he did not yet know enough to write the story of Niño's corruption. Playing to his strong suit, Hemingway refocused the novel on the Paris crowd.

The result is a novel about the corruption of Jake Barnes, whose hopeless love for Brett leads him to pimp away his membership in Montoya's select club of *afición*. As he leaves Pamplona, Jake, with typical understatement, tells us, "We had lunch and paid the bill. Montoya did not come near us. One of the maids brought the bill" (228). Implicit in these lines is the impossibility of Jake's ever returning to Pamplona. No wonder he makes such bitter comments when he is alone at San Sebastian; no wonder he gets drunk in Madrid when rescuing Brett. Jake Barnes has destroyed one of the last values left him in an already impoverished world.

Jake's final condition frequently escapes the contemporary reader, who lacks the historical context for reading the novel. If one misses the ironic and understated references, it may not seem like "such a hell of a sad story" as it did to Hemingway. Unless one understands the moral background of the period, one may find the Latin Quarter life nostalgically romantic and fail to see the reflection of America self-destructing in the twenties. The blithe reader may see Cohn as the cause of all the troubles. It was not Cohn; it was the times. It was Jake Barnes, impotent in more ways than one, caught in his times, his value system jerked from beneath his feet. He is, finally, the prewar man stripped of all defenses, bereft of values, seduced and abandoned by his times. If at Botin's he gets a bit drunk listening to Brett, perhaps we can forgive him, for both the reader and Jake realize that he is a most ineffectual man in a most unpromising place.

NOTES

1. EH–Ernest Walsh, January 2, 1926, in Carlos Baker, ed., *Ernest Hemingway: Selected Letters,* (New York: Scribners, 1981), p. 186.
2. Herbert S. Gorman, November 14, 1926, in Robert O. Stephens, ed., *Ernest Hemingway, The Critical Reception* (New York: Burt Franklin, 1977), p. 38.
3. Baker, ed., *Selected Letters,* p. 199.
4. EH–Scott Fitzgerald, c. May 20, 1926, Baker, ed., *Selected Letters,* pp. 204–5.
5. EH–Max Perkins, November 16, 1926, Baker, ed., *Selected Letters,* pp. 225–6.
6. Baker, ed., *Selected Letters,* p. 212.
7. Item 202c, Hemingway Archive, Kennedy Library, as cited in Frederic Svoboda, *Hemingway and The Sun Also Rises* (Lawrence: University Press of Kansas, 1983), p. 106.
8. Stephens, ed., *The Critical Reception,* p. 37.
9. "Clinical Notes," *American Mercury* 3 (September–December 1924):57.
10. *The New Republic* (June 28, 1922), p. 118.
11. James M. Cain, "Politician: Female," *American Mercury* 3 (September–December 1924):277.
12. Reprinted in Svoboda, *Hemingway,* p. 135.
13. "American Bohemians in Paris," March 25, 1922, *Toronto Star Weekly,* reprinted in *By-Line Ernest Hemingway,* ed. William White (New York: Scribners, 1967), pp. 23–5.
14. See my "False Dawn: A Preliminary Analysis of *The Sun Also Rises* Manuscript," in *Hemingway: A Revaluation,* ed. Donald R. Noble (Troy, N.Y.: Whitson, 1983), pp. 115–34.
15. Ibid., p. 128; permission originally granted by Mary Hemingway and the Kennedy Library.

4

Brett Ashley as New Woman in *The Sun Also Rises*

WENDY MARTIN

THE *Sun Also Rises*, published in the autumn of 1926, became, along with *The Great Gatsby*, published the previous year, the novel that captured the excitement of the jazz age and expatriate glamour as well as the cultural dislocation and psychological malaise that were the legacy of World War I. The emotional upheavals of Jake Barnes and Brett Ashley, and their friends Bill Gorton, Mike Campbell, and Robert Cohn, who live episodically, taking risks and contending with the elation or despair that follows in the wake of their adventures, provide a cartography of the experience of the lost generation.[1] In this novel filled with surface excitement – love, sexual rivalry, café hopping in France, the revelry of the festival of San Fermin in Pamplona, fishing excursions in the Spanish countryside – Brett and Jake emerge as the paradigmatic couple who best represent the shift in the perception of gender following World War I. This redefinition of masculinity and femininity was not an abrupt rift in the cultural landscape but rather a gradual shifting of the ground on which the edifice of Victorian sexual identity was built.

The blending of the polarized spheres that traditionally separated the lives of women and men was, in part, the result of the centrifugal swirl of events following World War I. As Paul Fussell has observed in *The Great War and Modern Memory*, 8 million soldiers died in the trenches of Western Europe in the years 1914–18, and this massive carnage created a generation of men for whom the concepts of glorious battle, honor, and heroism became either suspect or a mockery.[2] Hemingway himself said:

> I was an awful dope when I went into the last war, I can remember
> just thinking that we were the home team and the Austrians were
> the visiting team.[3]

Like John Peal Bishop, E. E. Cummings, John Dos Passos, and
Dashiell Hammett, Hemingway joined the ambulance corps, which
Malcolm Cowley described as "a college extension course for a
generation of writers."[4] In Italy, Hemingway was wounded in a
trench by an Austrian mortar, a man next to him was killed in-
stantly, and another was wounded critically. This random, imper-
sonal violence undermined notions of the romance of war and the
belief in the battlefield as the proving ground for courage; Hemingway observed, "There are no heroes in this war . . . All the heroes
are dead."[5] In *The Sun Also Rises* Hemingway makes it clear that
the postwar sensibility as exemplified by Jake is one of severe loss,
emasculation, and impotence. In contrast to Robert Cohn's anachronistic readiness to fight to protect his honor or defend his lady
from insults, Jake feels tricked by the war and is dismayed at
having been a pawn in an international con game masterminded
by bankers and politicians. Expressing Hemingway's disillusionment, Frederic Henry observes in *A Farewell to Arms*, published
three years after *The Sun Also Rises:*

> I did not say anything. I was always embarrassed by the words
> sacred, glorious, and sacrifice and the expression in vain. We had
> heard them, sometimes standing in the rain almost out of earshot,
> so that only the shouted words came through, and had read them
> on proclamations that were slapped up by billposters over other
> proclamations, now for a long time, and I had seen nothing sacred,
> and the things that were glorious had no glory and the sacrifices
> were like the stock yards at Chicago if nothing was done with the
> meat except to bury it.[6]

With the loss of the conviction of masculine invincibility and
authority after the war came a stoic attitude that is a compensatory
stance for this new awareness of vulnerability. Hemingway's definition of courage, which he succinctly phrased as "grace under
pressure," is in many respects a startling echo of the Victorian
adage to "suffer and be still" that was directed to women who felt
helpless to meet the demands of their sacrificial role. Just as the
true woman was self-effacing in the name of familial and social

stability, the ideal man of Hemingway's world consciously suppressed his feelings, thereby neutralizing his response in the name of courage or mastery and the need to protect his country. But the stoicism and willed mastery are seen as an obligation or a challenge to be met consciously rather than as a natural — that is to say, habitual — response. Certainly this form of willed courage is not glorious, nor is it even a prerogative; instead it is a necessity born out of the need to conceal masculine vulnerability and loss of certainty.

A further parallel between the psychic cost of the redemptive role of Victorian women and the disequilibrium of the war-weary man of the lost generation can be seen in the extreme in their respective pathologies — hysteria and shell shock. Both are somatic responses to psychological conflicts; hysteria is a female response to the inability to reconcile the need for self-expression and the cultural imperative for self-denial, and shell shock is a parallel response of men who are terrified of combat and death on the battlefield. Interestingly, hysteria is a response to excessive domestic *confinement* and shell shock to excessive *exposure*. Yet both of these extremes produce the same range of symptoms — including exhaustion, confusion, speech defects, blindness, deafness, and paralysis.

In the gap of meaning that opened after World War I, the female role was undergoing a transformation in the popular consciousness from passive, private creature to avid individualist in pursuit of new experiences. The housebound Victorian nurturer was becoming the modern woman of unprecedented mobility and public visibility. Traditionally, women have inhabited private spaces, which are simultaneously protected and claustrophobic. Along with the opportunities created by the dissolution of polarized social spheres came increased vulnerability for women. Because public space is defined as male, women were often seen either as interlopers or as "fair game" undeserving of respect or safety. Frequently a woman who left the sanctity of the home was automatically defined as disreputable or dangerous.

Although the highly glamorized flapper seen dancing, smoking, and drinking in public and consorting with men of her own choice in cafés and dancehalls was largely a media phenomenon, the image of the short-skirted, shimmying, seductive, sleek femininity promised unprecedented freedom for twentieth-century women in general. Emphasis on mobility and active participation in public life for women in the 1920s — the first decade in which women had the vote — seemed to represent a dramatic break with the past; but in fact, the postwar decade actually consolidated the gains that had been achieved by feminists over a period of almost 100 years.

In the late nineteenth century the new woman, like the modern woman of the 1920s, was a product of the urban life of the developing industrial cities. She was educated, valued her autonomy, and did not automatically subscribe to the values of the family; frequently, she was single and had a career. No longer did she define herself as a domestic being; openly rebelling against nineteenth-century bourgeois priorities, the new woman rejected traditional feminine ideals of purity, piety, and submission. Instead she insisted on reproductive freedom, self-expression, and a voice in public life. In short, the new woman rebelled against patriarchal marriage and, protesting against a social order that was rooted in female biology, she refused to play the role of the ethereal other. Since her demands for personal fulfillment suggested a need for new emotional arrangements, they were seen as threatening the social order.

The war had given a generation of women like Sylvia Beach an opportunity to test their abilities; service in the nursing or agricultural corps taught women not only that they could work effectively but that their work was valuable. This postwar feminist consciousness was especially evident in Paris in the early 1920s, when there were more than eighty feminist societies with a total of more than 60,000 members. This emphasis on women's freedom is demonstrated by the 1922 publication of the best-selling novel *Garcon* by Victor Margueritte, about a nineteen-year-old unmarried woman who plans to have a baby and raise it independently of patriarchal society.[7]

The new woman's radical challenge to the traditional social structure is seen in Lady Brett Ashley, who has stepped off the pedestal and now roams the world. Entering the public sphere without apology, she dares to frequent places and events previously off limits to her, such as the bar and the bullfight. Gone are the long skirts, bustles, and constricted waists: New clothes designed by Coco Chanel and Erté are intended for movement. The short skirts and light fabrics of the new fashions for women shocked traditionalists. In the spring of 1925, the *New York Times* reported that a woman wearing a dress with transparent sleeves literally caused a riot in London. When she was arrested for indecent exposure and disturbing the peace, the woman protested that such dresses were the fashion in New York City. Similarly, when Brett appears with bare shoulders in Montoya's bar in Pamplona, she deeply offends him; her exposed flesh marks her as a fallen woman.

In spite of the fact that Brett tries to break free of patriarchal control, she often vacillates between the extremes of self-abnegation and self-indulgence, and her relationships with her two former husbands, as well as with Mike Campbell, Robert Cohn, and even Jake, are filled with ambivalence, anxiety, and frequently alienation. Although Brett has the distinction of having married into the British aristocracy, her protected social status has proved to be inversely proportional to her personal satisfaction. As she bitterly observes, "I had such a hell of a happy life with the British aristocracy."[8] As she tries to find her way between the Scylla of social constraint and the Charybdis of chaotic freedom, her search for a new direction is not validated by the social world in which she lives. In spite of Hemingway's sympathetic treatment of Brett, much critical reaction has mirrored traditional values: Allen Tate calls her "hard-boiled"; Theodore Bardake sees her as a "woman devoid of womanhood"; Jackson Benson says that she is "a female who never becomes a woman"; Edmund Wilson describes her as "an exclusively destructive force"; and John Aldridge declares that Brett is a "compulsive bitch."[9] In a somewhat more generous interpretation, Roger Whitlow describes Brett as self-destructive, and Delbert Wylder sees her as a Janus-like character.[10]

Brett's loose, disordered relationships reflect the shattered unity and contradictions of the modern world. On the one hand, she is insouciant, careless, a femme fatale – a woman dangerous to men; on the other, she reflexively lapses into the role of redemptive woman by trying to save men through her sexuality. Mike observes that Brett "loves looking after people" (203), and she has an affair with Robert Cohn because she feels sorry for him and hopes that a romantic interlude will lift his spirits. When he persists in playing the knight who wants to rescue his damsel in distress, she scorns him for his inability to accept episodic or casual sex. In many respects, Brett represents Hemingway's idealized rendering of the woman free of sexual repression. Following F. Scott Fitzgerald's advice, Hemingway cut the original fifteen-page opening sequence of *The Sun Also Rises,* in which he made it clear that the novel was about Brett. The original opening of the novel begins: "This is a novel about a lady. Her name is Lady Ashley and when the story begins she is living in Paris and it is spring."[11]

In the 1920s, Freud's theories of repression were used to justify free love.[12] Contradicting traditional theories of sexuality in the 1920s based on male sexual drive and female receptivity, Brett represents the principle of female eros unbounded by patriarchal control; her closest friend and "true love" is a man who is physically impotent due to a war wound. Many critics have equated Jake's sexual disability with Hemingway's fear of inadequacy, but Jakes affliction has more cultural than biographical significance.[13] His sexual impotence is a sign of loss of masculine power and authority and the axiomatic right to exercise social control. Since Jake's war wound has made it impossible for him to make a physical claim on Brett, he is the only man in the novel who does not try to possess her.

One of the important observations about sexual politics in the novel is that masculine eroticism confines women; therefore, Hemingway implies that sex and friendship are inversely related. In traditional courtship situations, the woman's power is the power to be pursued; once caught, she forfeits her opportunity to choose. Here there are parallels with economic processes; by retaining the interest of multiple suitors, Brett keeps her options open, diversifies her investment of social and sexual energy, and thereby maximizes her opportunities.

Interestingly, Brett breaks up her relationships when her lovers attempt to claim her, that is, to exercise authority over her. She even leaves the bullfighter Romero — a man to whom she is overwhelmingly attracted — when he shows signs of wanting to domesticate her: He tells her to give up her mannish felt hat, to let her hair grow long, to wear more modest clothes. But she has rejected the ideal of female dependence and delicacy: "He wanted me to grow my hair out. Me, with long hair. I'd look so like hell" (242).

Brett prides herself on her daring; for example, she is exceptional in her willingness to take sexual risks. Nevertheless, she is still caught between two modes of gender representation: that of the idealized woman on the pedestal and that of the self-reliant modern woman. She is both the idealized other whom men seek as a prize for their prowess and the autonomous woman who tries to make her own decisions. Although she has broken the connection between moral and physical purity, she still plays the redemptive role of trying to save men through her sexuality – the modern counterpart of Victorian feminine spirituality. In spite of the fact that she is no longer confined to the claustrophobic patriarchal house that in nineteenth-century feminist iconography was the place of entrapment, like the jazz age flapper she has not yet (nor have her male counterparts, for that matter) redefined the traditional relationships of sex and money. Brett has some money from her second husband, from whom she has separated; she also depends on her ability to attract men who will pay for her drinks, her dinners, her taxis and trains. And just as she expects men to pay for many of her pleasures, most of the men in the novel are also bound by the traditional code to assume financial responsibility for women in exchange for their attention. If Brett has gained a measure of freedom in leaving the traditional household, she is still very much dependent on men, who provide an arena in which she can be attractive and socially active as well as financially secure.

Brett's lack of financial and psychological independence is clearly stated in the opening paragraphs of the novel; Hemingway observes that Brett has a "grand vitality" but that she "has never been very good at being alone." Her lack of judgment about her romantic liaisons is evident in the following paragraph from the unpublished beginning:

> Lady Ashley was born Elizabeth Brett Murray. Her title came from her second husband. She had divorced one husband for some-

thing or other, mutual consent; not until after he had put one of
those notices in the papers stating that after this date he would not
be responsible for any debts, etc. He was a Scotchman and found
Brett much too expensive, especially as she had only married him to
get rid of him and to get away from home. At present she had a legal
separation from her second husband, who had the title, because he
was a dipsomaniac, he having learned it in the North Sea commanding a mine-sweeper, Brett said. When he had gotten to be a
proper thoroughgoing dipsomaniac and found that Brett did not
love him he tried to kill her, and between times slept on the floor
and was never sober and had great spells of crying. Brett always
declared that it had been one of the really great mistakes of her life
to have married a sailor. She should have known better, she said,
but she had sent the one man she had wanted to marry off to
Mesopotamia so he would last out the war, and he had died of some
very unromantic form of dysentery and she certainly could not
marry Jake Barnes, so when she had to marry she had married Lord
Robert Ashley, who proceeded to become a dipsomaniac as before
stated.[14]

In her exchange of sexual and psychological attention with men
in return for their financial favors and protection, Brett mirrors
both the traditional wife and the prostitute. Yet she will be neither
– she will not submit to the authority or the direction of men, nor
will she take money in payment for sex because that would be
prostitution. In this transition among wife, mistress, and free
woman, Brett and the other women in this novel – Frances,
Georgette, and Edna – sometimes find themselves in awkward
and contradictory roles.[15] Interestingly, radical feminists and pros-
titutes themselves have argued that marriage is a sanctioned exchange of sex and nurturance for financial protection and social
status and that this basic economic transaction is obscured by
sentimental ideology, but Brett shields herself from that knowledge. Although she chooses willed ignorance, she does manage to
challenge successfully the male control of female eros.

Hemingway gives considerable attention to financial matters in
The Sun Also Rises; in this novel, money and morality are closely
intertwined. Both Jake and the count, who has been in "seven
wars and four revolutions" (60) and has arrow wounds to prove
it, share the conviction that the confrontation with death has in-

tensified their appreciation of life. By paying the ultimate price —
risking death — they have earned the right to appreciate life. As the
Count remarks:

> "You see, Mr. Barnes, it is because I have lived very much that now
> I can enjoy everything so well. Don't you find it like that?"
> "Yes, absolutely."
> "I know," said the Count. "That is the secret. You must get to know
> the values." (p. 60)

Brett, who has less experience, less money, and therefore less
control over the circumstances of her life, questions this economic
reductionism: "Doesn't anything ever happen to your values?"
The count, who is buffered by both his wide experience and his
considerable fortune, answers, "No, not any more" (61). His financial and emotional priorities are established, and he has even
factored in the cost of falling in love. Aptly titled, the count esti-
mates the cost — psychological as well as economic — of his experiences and consciously decides what price he is willing to pay. So,
economic independence and psychological freedom are correlated,
and it is the men in this novel who control most of the money.

In an often quoted passage from the novel, Jake articulates his
version of this market economy of the emotions, which paradox-
ically leads him to observe that the financial and social compensation for men and women is dramatically different. Interestingly,
this quantification of pleasure yields a new understanding of the
double standard, which he comes to realize is like getting a loan
with an unspecified repayment date:

> I had been having Brett for a friend. I had not been thinking about
> her side of it. I had been getting something for nothing. That only
> delayed the presentation of the bill. The bill always came. That was
> one of the swell things you could count on.
> I thought I had paid for everything. Not like the woman who pays
> and pays. No idea of retribution or punishment. Just exchange of
> values. You gave up something and got something else or you
> worked for something. You paid some way for everything that was
> any good. I paid my way into things that I liked, so that I had a good
> time. Either you paid by learning about them or by experience, or
> by taking chances, or by money. Enjoying living was learning to get
> your money's worth and knowing when you had it. (p. 148)[16]

In contrast to the Scottish aristocrat Mike Campbell, whose entire existence is sustained by debt financing, Jake believes in fiscal and emotional responsibility. Yet he has miscalculated the cost of Brett's lifestyle, and he must ultimately accept the financial and social compromises necessary for her to survive in a rapidly changing world, as well as her effort to forge an individual identity that includes sexual freedom. Jake understands that to be her friend, he must truly relinquish his desire to control her. Because Jake is able to wrestle with this issue of territoriality and possessiveness and to accept his loss of control, he is the only man in the novel who is able to meet Brett on common ground.

In part, Jake's philosophy represents a wary response to a historical period when credit was available for the first time on a large scale, and when there was a concerted effort by the government and financial institutions to encourage people to consume, not to save. In response to the threat to capitalist values posed by the Russian Revolution of 1917, American banking and business interests made a concerted effort to create easy credit. With this increased availability of money, the consumer market expanded and the stock market soared in response to widespread speculation that the economy would grow even stronger. All classes of people participated in the speculative fire that ignited Wall Street, and when the flames were doused in 1929, margin calls were delivered to chauffeurs and chambermaids along with bankers and brokers.

A profound – if human – exchange between Jake and his friend Bill Gorton underscores the far-reaching implications of this new wave of capitalism that depends on the consumption of manufactured goods produced by the industrial economies of the United States and Western Europe. While strolling the streets of Paris, Bill wants to buy a stuffed dog: "Mean everything in the world to you after you bought it," he tells Jake. "Simple exchange of values. You give them money. They give you a stuffed dog." When Jake resists, Bill retorts, "All right. Have it your way. Road to hell paved with unbought stuffed dogs. Not my fault" (72–3).

During 1924–6, while *The Sun Also Rises* was written and published, the dollar value in francs made it possible for American writers to live quite well in France on limited budgets, and the heirs of wealthy American families – Harry and Caresse Crosby,

Sara and Gerald Murphy, for example – had an extensive staff of servants, drank the finest wines, and traveled widely. Post–World War I Paris was a haven not only for American expatriates but for refugees and émigrés from all over the world. The disillusioned as well as the disenfranchised flocked to the City of Light. This period of social upheaval was accompanied by an extraordinary artistic ferment: The dadaists celebrated the sense of absurdity and pos- sibility of these tumultuous times. The cafés and ateliers were filled with artists and intellectuals whose work formed the cornerstone of modern art, including Chagall, Cocteau, Diagilev, Dos Passos, Fitzgerald, Gurdjieff, James Joyce, Hemingway, Picabia, Ezra Pound, Man Ray, Satie, Stravinsky, and Tzara. The *années folles,* the crazy years, as the French described the decade, were exciting for women as well as for men. Participating in every aspect of artistic life – dance, painting, photography, writing – as well as in politics, many women experienced unprecedented opportunities, among them Bernice Abbot, Josephine Baker, Djuna Barnes, Natalie Barney, Sylvia Beach, Kay Boyle, Nancy Cunard, Isadora Duncan, Janet Flanner, Emma Goldman, Mina Loy, Katherine Mansfield, and Gertrude Stein.

In *The Sun Also Rises,* the emotional challenges of Brett and Jake are antithetical: Jake must learn to accept the discomfort and un- certainty that come with his loss of authority, and Brett must learn to make choices for herself and to take responsibility for those choices. In this reworking of traditional psychological patterns, Jake becomes more nurturing and *responsive,* Brett more decisive and *responsible.* This role reversal reflects the changing definitions of gender in the jazz age. In *The Sun Also Rises,* men cry and women swear; Brett aggressively expresses her sexual desires, while her lovers wait to be chosen; she likes action – noisy public gatherings, large parties, the blood and gore of the bullfight – whereas the men appreciate the pleasure of sipping brandy in a quiet café.

The loss of traditional cultural meaning is accompanied by a loss of certainty about proper feminine and masculine behavior. Since gender is a social construction, new roles represent a response to new realities, and through trial and error, new forms of sexual behavior emerge. New configurations of gender shatter the old frame, and stripped of their traditional roles, the characters in *The Sun Also Rises* are more transparent, that is, more able to express a greater range of feelings.

Although Hemingway is often stereotyped as a machismo writer, he was fascinated with the variability of the human sexual response and its extraordinary range of expression. Even though Hemingway cultivated a traditional masculine personal and literary style – he was called "Poppa" and much of his work focuses on hunting, fishing, boxing, and bullfighting – he also experimented with role reversal in lovemaking with his wives and wrote a novel and short stories emphasizing androgynous behavior.

In "The Garden of Eden," an unpublished novel manuscript now housed in the Kennedy Library, Hemingway explores the variations of gender identity in terms that echo Brett's disagreement with Romero about her short hair and mannish hat. As in Virginia Woolf's *Orlando,* characters reverse roles: Katherine announces that she wants to become a man and cuts her hair short; she urges her lover, David, to become a woman, or at the very least she wants them to become brothers. David is fascinated and frightened by Katherine's insistence on sexual experimentation. Another couple, Nick and Barbara, both grow their hair long and explore their feminine capacities. This 1,214-page manuscript is set in a small fishing village in the south of France when Hemingway and his second wife, Pauline, honeymooned in 1927 and contains numerous references to experimental lovemaking, never specified but described as "shameless."[17]

Another unpublished story, "A Story of a Man Who Always Wanted to Have Long Hair," indicates that Hemingway continued to be interested in androgynous sexuality, as does an observation by his last wife, Mary:

> In our mutual sensory delights we were smoothly interlocking parts of a single entity, the big cogwheel and the smaller cogwheel. . . . Maybe we were androgynous.[18]

In contrast to his private sexual experiments, the public Hemingway represented tough masculinity, so much so that Zelda Fitzgerald told him that nobody could be that masculine. In an essay in the *New Republic* in 1933, Max Eastman derided Hemingway as "wearing false hair on his chest." Enraged by Eastman's remark, Hemingway stormed into the *New Republic*'s office to display his own hairy chest and then ripped open Eastman's shirt to reveal a hairless chest. Although Hemingway responded with fury when anyone dared to impugn has masculinity, he was a nurturing person. According to Sylvia Beach, he was an unusually loving father and did "everything but breastfeed his baby."[19]

In the context of the new cultural openness – with its new range of ontological possibilities – both Brett and Jake believe in *risk* as the measure of the importance of a choice or action. The true risk taker – the aficionado – is one who is willing to walk the line between life and death in the pursuit of meaning. Yet *afición* – passion – also means certain suffering. For Jake, *afición* is a commitment without reservation to the dangers of the bullfight, and for him, Pedro Romero is the heroic exemplar of masculine courage in his willingness to face the bull without reservation, without protection: "Romero had the old thing, the holding of his purity of line through the maximum of exposure" (168). But Romero is a *boy;* he is nineteen and not yet fully aware of the meaning or dangers of the risks he takes. He is protected, in part, by his innocence.

Brett's affairs represent the kind of risk taking for her that the confrontation with the bull represents for Romero; by exercising sexual freedom she risks disease, pregnancy, ostracism. Brett's freedom of choice leads to what I would call an anxiety of opportunity, and her response is regressive. Ironically, in spite of her many options, when she does choose for herself, she selects Romero, a traditional man in the person of a nineteen-year-old bullfighter. Although Brett has chosen Romero for deeply personal reasons (she explains to Jake, "I've got to do something I really want to do. I've lost my self-respect" [183]), she recognizes that with this choice comes certain suffering. As she phrases it, "I'm a goner" (183). But this female version of romantic agony is based on the capacity to endure pain. And her final triumph in this scenario of self-denial is to relinquish Romero.

Hemingway's pastoral interludes, in which his male characters seek relief from social tensions, are part of a tradition in American fiction that begins with Cooper and Brackenridge and extends through Hawthorne, Melville, and Twain. In rural settings, fictional characters are free from the demands of horological time and linear consciousness. Hemingway's description of the excursion to the Irati River expresses this sense of harmonious ease; nature is not divided into artificial hierarchical categories and is instead described as an unbroken whole. The fishing trip in *The Sun Also Rises* is a rite of purification for Jake and Bill: It represents a release from social and sexual competition, an anodyne to the stress of café society. Like Huck Finn, who heads for the woods to escape the confinement of the Widow Douglas's drawing room, Bill and Jake go to the country to escape social constraints. Not only is there freedom from schedules – "Wonderful how one loses track of the days up here in the mountains" (127) – there is freedom from the traditional inhibition of masculine emotion: "Listen. You're a hell of a good guy, and I'm fonder of you than anybody on earth. I couldn't tell you that in New York. It'd mean I was a faggot," Bill declares to Jake (116).

The Irati River, where the two men fish for trout, is described in idealized terms:

> The road came out from the shadow of the woods into the hot sun. Ahead was the river valley. Beyond the river was a steep hill. There was a field of buckwheat on the hill. We saw a white house under the trees on the hillside. It was very hot and we stopped under some trees beside the river. (p. 118).

Here nature and civilization harmoniously coexist. No single feature of the landscape dominates; the house nestles into the hillside and does not command the heights. This passage, then, creates a mood of tranquility, of restful stasis. In reality, the event on which this fishing expedition was based was quite different. Hemingway and his friend visited the Irati, only to discover that loggers had dumped debris into the river, leaving it clogged and muddy.[20]

In spite of freedom, however temporary, from emotional and social tensions, Jake and Bill descend from the mountains and return to the fiesta at Pamplona. This celebration provides the same release for the peasants of the area that fishing on the Irati River does for Jake and Bill, but the patterns are reversed: The peasants come to the city to seek relief from working the land, just as Jake and Bill retreat to the country to rest from urban tensions. This pattern recapitulates the larger historical movement from land to city to land again. In both cases, it is a retreat from responsibility and daily cares that is sought.

In contrast to the appeal of pastoral tranquility to the men, Brett knows that it is the urban centers that provide mobility and choices for the new woman, not the country with its traditionally limited vision of woman as reproductive being. In an emblematic moment when Jake asks Brett, "Couldn't we go off in the country for a while?", she responds, "It wouldn't do any good. I'll go if you like. But I couldn't live quietly in the country. Not with my own true love." Brett is riding a historical wave and Jake responds, "I know" (55).

At moments like this, Jake represents the desire to remain grounded in familiar traditions, established economic and social rituals. He doesn't like credit, debit financing, unusual sexual arrangements. Yet his penchant for risk taking is a psychological representation of an economic mode. Living on the edge is like buying on margin: It is unpredictable, potentially dangerous, exhilarating, frightening. Both margin buying and a risk-oriented life create the possibility of having more resources − whether money or a wealth of experiences − and carry with them the risk of financial collapse like the crash of 1929 or emotional collapse like F. Scott Fitzgerald's as described in *The Crack-Up*.[21]

The manuscript of *The Sun Also Rises* indicate that Hemingway identified himself with Jake, who was called Hem or Ernie in the early drafts.[22] During the writing of this novel, Hemingway was financially supported by his wife Hadley, and the considerable anxiety caused by his financial dependence on her is expressed in the character of Jake. Just as Nathaniel Hawthorne, who was supported by his wife Sophia while writing *The Scarlet Letter*, expressed his tensions regarding the limits and responsibilities of gender roles in the characters of Hester and Dimmesdale, so Hemingway expresses the same concerns via Jake and Brett. In both novels, the female protagonists threaten to overpower the men they love; in both novels, the men feel ambivalent about their attraction to these unusual women and sometimes unmanned, demeaned in the face of demands made on them. Hawthorne resolves the tensions in *The Scarlet Letter* by returning to tradition: Hester does not escape social constraints and judgment; her role is to counsel future generations of women to avoid her mistakes. Hawthorne tells us that his wife was deeply disturbed by the fact that Hester Prynne was not punished more severely for her transgression, and it is possible that Hawthorne added the final paragraphs of *The Scarlet Letter* to appease Sophia. But Hemingway takes another route; he does not relegate Brett to the domestic realm. By leaving his heroine free and relatively intact both emotionally and physically, he disengages from the tradition of the destruction of the female protagonist in American fiction from *Charlotte Temple* to *The House of Mirth* and *The Awakening*.

Brett's statement at the conclusion of the novel, "we would have had such a damned good time together," and Jake's response, "Isn't it pretty to think so?" (247), have partly biographical, partly historical origins. After concluding *The Sun Also Rises*, Hemingway divorced Hadley in order to marry the very wealthy Pauline Pfeiffer, with whom he went on fishing expeditions and safaris.[23] In sharp contrast to Hawthorne, who needed the protective sanctity of his home and the gentle ministrations of Sophia, Hemingway left his domestic life (and felt *extremely* guilty about doing so) in order to live a more exciting and adventurous existence. The conclusion of *The Sun Also Rises* reflects his conviction that there was no going back for him and, for that matter, no turning back the tide of history for the new woman *and* the new man. Jake and Brett want to want the dream of pastoral simplicity and domestic harmony – but, in fact, they don't.

In spite of the fact that traditional ideals are rejected in this novel, *The Sun Also Rises* concludes with an abatement of tensions between Brett and Jake that is the beginning of genuine friendship. As Jake and Brett toast each other with their "coldly beaded" glasses, they experience the deep mutuality that Bill and Jake share when they drink from the "moisture beaded" wine bottles that had been cooled in the Irati River. Significantly, Brett and Jake do not discover this mutuality in idealized pastoral space; instead, they acknowledge each other as emotional equals while enjoying the civility of the bar in the Palace Hotel in Madrid. This sharing of public space signals the possibility of new kinds of relationships for women and men in the twentieth century.

NOTES

1. Malcom Cowley, *Exile's Return: A Literary Odyssey of the 1920s* (New York: Viking, 1951), p. 39, observes that the World War I years caused his generation to "fear boredom more than death."
2. Paul Fussell, *The Great War and Modern Memory* (New York: Oxford University Press, 1975), p. 13.
3. Carlos Baker, *Ernest Hemingway, A Life Story* (New York: Scribners, 1969), p. 8.
4. Cowley, *Exile's Return*, p. 13.
5. Baker, *Ernest Hemingway*, p. 52.
6. Ernest Hemingway, *A Farewell to Arms* (New York: Scribners, 1929), pp. 184–5.
7. William Wiser, *The Crazy Years: Paris in the Twenties* (New York: G. K. Hall, 1983), p. 85.
8. Ernest Hemingway, *The Sun Also Rises* (New York: Scribners, 1926), p. 203. All subsequent citations of this novel appear in the text itself. Hemingway modeled Brett Ashley on Lady Duff Twysden, who was with his group in Pamplona in the summer of 1925. See, for example, Bertram D. Sarason, "Lady Brett Ashley and Lady Duff Twysden," *Connecticut Review* 2 (1969):5–13.
9. Allen Tate, "Hard Boiled," *The Merrill Studies in The Sun Also Rises*, ed. William White (Columbus, Ohio: Charles E. Merrill, 1969), p. 18; Theodore Bardacke, "Hemingway's Women," *Ernest Hemingway: The Man and His Work*, ed. John K. M. McCaffery (New York: Avon, 1950), p. 309; Jackson Benson, *Hemingway: The Writer's Art of Self-Defense* (Minneapolis: University of Minnesota Press, 1969), p. 30; Edmund Wilson, *The Wound and the Bow* (Cambridge, Mass.: Houghton Mifflin, 1941), p. 238; John W. Aldridge, *After the Lost Generation* (New York: McGraw-Hill, 1951), p. 24.
10. Delbert E. Wylder, "The Two Faces of Brett: The Role of the New Woman in *The Sun Also Rises*," *Kentucky Philological Association Bulletin* (1980):23–33.
11. Ernest Hemingway, "The Unpublished Opening of *The Sun Also Rises*" *Antaeus* 33 (Spring, 1979):7.
12. Paul Johnson, *Modern Times: The World from the Twenties to the Eighties* (New York: Harper & Row, 1983), pp. 5–10.

13. Philip Young, in *Ernest Hemingway: A Reconsideration* (Philadelphia: University of Pennsylvania Press, 1966), argues that Hemingway's wounded heroes express his pathological preoccupation with death and his recurrent need to discharge his fear of death through vicarious killing and dying.

14. Hemingway, "Unpublished Opening," 7.

15. F. Scott Donaldson, *By Force of Will: The Life and Art of Ernest Hemingway* (New York: Viking, 1977), p. 25, argues that "it is women like Brett . . . who provide unfair competition to the streetwalkers of Paris."

16. For a discussion of money in the novel, see Richard P. Sugg, "Hemingway, Money, and *The Sun Also Rises*," *Fitzgerald–Hemingway Annual* (1972):245–55.

17. Aaron Latham, "Machismo," *New York Times* Sunday Magazine, October 16, 1977, p. 81.

18. Ibid., p. 89.

19. Noel Riley Fitch, *Sylvia Beach and the Lost Generation* (New York: Norton, 1983), p. 166.

20. Fredric Joseph Svoboda, *Hemingway and* The Sun Also Rises: *The Crafting of a Style* (Lawrence: University Press of Kansas, 1983), p. 215.

21. F. Scott Fitzgerald, *The Crack-Up*, ed. Edmund Wilson (New York: J. Laughlin, 1945).

22. Svoboda, *Hemingway*, p. 9.

23. For general background about Hemingway's guilt and anxiety about this impending divorce, see *Sara and Gerald: Villa America and After* (New York: Holt, Rinehart & Winston, 1984), pp. 23–5.

Decoding the Hemingway Hero in
The Sun Also Rises

ARNOLD E. AND CATHY N. DAVIDSON

"Maybe a story is better without any hero."
−From an early draft of *The Sun Also Rises*[1]

1

DESPITE its increasing currency in literary debate, the term "deconstruction" still prompts in many readers a sense of apprehension and unease. Partly it is a matter of critical language: Much deconstructive criticism turns, like the term itself, on neologisms designed to address new critical concerns in new ways. The unversed reader, like a tourist in a foreign land, longs for a familiar idiom or at least a phrasebook. Partly it is a matter of critical stance: The deconstructive critic often posits different relationships between critic and text, between writer and reader, from those presumed and explored by previous criticism. Nevertheless, and as Barbara Johnson has recently argued, the basic principles motivating the deconstructive enterprise are not radically different from those implicit in other types of criticism. As is suggested by the etymological root of the term itself, the primary task of criticism − from the Greek verb *krinein,* meaning to separate or choose − is to differentiate. According to Johnson, "The critic not only seeks to establish standards for evaluating the differences between texts, but also tries to preceive something uniquely different within each text he reads and in so doing to establish his own individual difference from other critics."[2] The deconstructive critic fully acknowledges the subjective aspect of reading a text (or writing one, for that matter), and, instead of attempting to make a particular reading seem somehow universal, emphasizes the *value* of individuality, plurality, subjectivity, and particularity in all responses to texts and in texts themselves. Instead of trying to resolve differences (of responses, perspectives, parts, whatever), the deconstructive critic attempts to exploit them. The aim is not to make the text speak with one paramount voice but to hear the different voices at play in the field of the text.

A history of the critical response to *The Sun Also Rises* suggests that this text should be particularly appreciated by the deconstructionist. For several generations now, critics have been constructing and deconstructing interpretations of Hemingway's first novel to produce a virtual industry of assessment and explication but no accepted, definitive reading of the work.[3] The deconstructionist would observe that such a wealth and range of responses is a tribute to the text itself. The novel can be deemed, in Roland Barthes's apt terminology, a "writerly" text – *le scriptible*, a work that allows the reader multiple entraces into and exits from it, myriad modes and methods of possible interpretation. Once more, "difference" is the issue, but we are primarily concerned now with the text's differences from itself and not with different readings of the same presumably monolithic text. Were *The Sun Also Rises*, for example, all of one piece – wholly consistent, univocal, "readerly," *le lisible* – there would be no need for us to interpret it again and again.[4] And there would be no occasion for the present volume either, for every reader should construct and "consume" essentially the same meaning from any perusal of the book. The reader's function, when engaging a readerly text, is essentially passive; in confronting *The Sun Also Rises*, however (and especially upon rereading it), the reader must cope with missing connections, contradictory value judgments, and textual inconsistencies. *Actively* engaging in the production of meaning out of such disparate elements, the reader even becomes, in at least a figurative sense, the text's writer.

One main purpose of deconstructive criticism, then, is to explore the "specificity of a text's critical difference from itself."[5] Looking especially for unspoken assumptions, hidden premises, and/or contradictions within the text, all of which leave it open to opposing responses, the deconstructive critic challenges the reductive model of interpretation. That challenge asks *why* it is desirable to posit unity as a primary feature of a literary work and at what cost this quality is pursued, discovered. Why reduce something as lively as the engaging text to, essentially, in T. S. Eliot's term, a formulation, a simple coda somehow concealed in the more complex and multifaceted text itself?

This last question has a particular point when applied to *The Sun Also Rises*, for much of the criticism of this novel represents an attempt to determine "the code" governing its hero. And then, going beyond this first code, critics have searched for the code of all Hemingway heroes, Hemingway fictions, and, beyond that, have also postulated connections between the code meaning of the fiction, Hemingway's famous laconic prose style, and the author's life.[6] But such a totalizing reading must somehow blink at its own inconsistencies. Jake, for example, clearly violates the code that, in the novel, most distinguishes him. His vaunted *afición* for the bull-fight ends with his failure in that service. And if we attempt to equate the Hemingway hero with Hemingway himself as hero – soldier, war correspondent, hunter, bare-chested boxer, and so forth – that equation stumbles over the pose implicit in the strained tone with which the personal assertions are typically advanced. A true Hemingway hero would never be guilty of Hemingway's persistent claims to herohood.

Furthermore, any equation of protagonist as hero and author as hero can run two ways, and thereby reduce *The Sun Also Rises* to a dubious roman à clef. Apparently Duff Twysden refused to sleep with Hemingway because he was married to Hadley and instead consorted (at least briefly) with another young novelist, Harold Loeb, all of which comes out rather differently in the novel.[7] But to translate marriage into emasculation and a petty personal jealousy into a pernicious form of anti-Semitism suggests neither code nor heroism. A rigorously readerly reading of *The Sun Also Rises* as a code novel forces us either, first, to overlook all features of the text (and/or the author) that do not affirm the code or are irrelevant to it; or, second, to feel disappointed by the breaches of the code and to condemn the book (and/or the author). These alternatives, incidentally, are dramatized in the novel through the character of Montoya, who first sees Jake as adhering to the code of *afición*, despite a few lapses from it, and then as unalterably, unforgivably outside the code. Either reading – of the character or the novel – compromises the other.

Nevertheless, much Hemingway criticism still judges Jake and the novel by a code first abstracted from the text and then reified by being differently applied to it – as if the code were absolute, an ostensibly external measure whereby the protagonist and his adventures could be fairly measured. This two-step procedure seems to us both dubious philosophy and dubious reading. The code has, of course, no a priori standing. Jake as success or Jake as failure – according to his adherence to or his fallings from the crucial code – is, in both cases, simply Jake caught in a circle of the critic's definition. To counter such definition and to show more fully how circular it finally is, we propose a different reading of the hero and the novel. Essentially, our argument is that the novel itself effectively refutes any standards in the novel whereby Jake might be either particularly praised or blamed.

2

Before proceeding with our own argument, however, we will briefly examine another critic's reading of another author's text. Roland Barthes's *S/Z*, his landmark study of Honoré de Balzac's short story "Sarrasine," provides us with both a model for and an introduction to our examination of Hemingway's *The Sun Also Rises*. To start with, and most important for our purposes, Barthes, instead of seeking any controlling key or code in Balzac's story, examines it in terms of different complementary and/or competing codes. He does so by splitting the text into 561 fragments and recording his response to each of these separate narrative bits. Through that dividing combined with his attendant responses, Barthes demonstrates how even a seemingly readerly nineteenth-century melodrama embodies self-contradictions that resist and refute any proffered unitary interpretation of the text.

The symbol, in Barthes's essay, for a multiplicity of meaning is the simple diacritical mark, /. This slash exemplifies the uneasy concatenation of unreconciled opposites that reside in any text (written or unwritten). To quote Barthes's own justification for his elision of "Sarrasine" to *S/Z*:

> It is fatal, the text says, to remove the dividing line, the paradigmatic slash mark which permits meaning to function (the wall of Antith-

esis), life to reproduce (the opposition of the sexes), property to be protected (rule of contract). . . . It is no longer possible to *represent*, to make things *representative*, individuated, separate, assigned; *Sarrasine* represents the very confusion of representation, the unbridled (pandemic) circulation of signs, of sexes, of fortunes.[8]

It comes down to either/or, but/and, black/white, and, above all, in Barthes's psychoanalytically informed semiotics, male/female. More to the point, it all comes down to /.

Or does it? Balzac's story, like *The Sun Also Rises*, revolves around questions of gender that are also both questions of surface (the prerogatives of gender) and questions of substance (the possession of gender). In "Sarrasine," the title character, a sculptor who specializes in idealized renditions of the female form, discovers the embodiment of his ideal woman in La Zambinella, an operatic soprano. Encountering this personification of his aesthetic and sexual fantasies, Sarrasine dichotomizes his destiny: "To be loved by her, or die!"[9] The dichotomies in the text, however, turn out to be considerably more complicated. To start with, Sarrasine's "her" is more accurately a "him," a castrati who, in keeping with the custom of the Italian opera of the time, merely plays the female roles. And yet Sarrasine does die for his ideal object, stabbed to death by the man who "keeps" La Zambinella and who also is — one of the obvious metaphors of the tale — another kind of "sculptor." As Barbara Johnson observes, the story constitutes, on a very profound level, a questioning and even a parody of all preconceptions of gender. In fact, Johnson takes Barthes to task for reducing the text (despite his 561 fragments) to a study of gender polarities when, in Johnson's reading, "Sarrasine" is not about gender polarities (assumptions about the fixed nature of male and female) but about the ways in which humans too simplistically reduce a whole range of characteristics (courage, beauty, dedication to art, sensitivity to art) to static notions of gender. In short, Barthes reverses what he sees as Balzac's definitions of gender, but Johnson insists that Balzac "deconstructs the very possibility of naming the difference" between genders and thus has "already in a sense done Barthes's work for him."[10]

Some parallels between Balzac's story and Hemingway's novel

should, at this point, be apparent. Of course, the sexual identities of the various characters in Hemingway's novel are freighted with different moral or psychological weight than in Balzac's story, yet the opposition between male/female, masculine/feminine, and (more particularized, more individualized) men/women is every bit as pervasive (the all-male ritual of the bullfight, the crucial matter of Jake's wound) and as undermined (Brett with her bob and her swagger, Romero with his grace and sensitivity, Jake with his manly principles but without his manhood) in one work as in the other. Both fictions also artificially inscribe the "natural differences" on which they turn to establish other paradigms around the destabilizing slash: artifice/nature, suggest/attest, free/formed, fiction/fact.

In the light of these parallels and paradigms, the facts of any fiction can begin to look uncertain indeed. Then again, uncertainty might be the best perspective for (or product of) a study of the text. But in either event, we herewith propose to subject *The Sun Also Rises* to a partially divisive reading around the dividing (and conjoining) slash. And although our model is largely based on Barthes's *S/Z,* our method is not. To start with, Balzac's short story can be printed in fragments throughout the book and then reprinted in its entirety as an appendix. That format does not lend itself to the analysis of longer works, and it is safe to say that there will never be a full Barthesian decoding of Tolstoi's *War and Peace* or even of Hemingway's *The Sun Also Rises.* Rather than divide Hemingway's novel into contiguous segments, as Barthes did with Balzac, we will assess only a sampling of sections from the text. Obviously, in the selection of these passages we have already made an interpretation. Critical attention is never arbitrary. But by our standards at least, we will look at some of the more overt code formulations in the book. And, second, in what is intended as an overview and introductory essay, we will not trace out the same full range of codes that Barthes considered but will concern ourselves mainly with passages in which questions of gender and value judgments associated with gender are central. Ranging these fragments and their implications oppositionally against one another, we propose to indicate how the novel sets forth at one and the same time a pervasive coding and decoding of heroic (read: prototypically male) behavior.

3

> Two taxis were coming down the steep street. . . . A crowd of young men, some in jerseys and some in their shirtsleeves, got out. I could see their hands and newly washed, wavy hair in the light from the door. The policeman standing by the door looked at me and smiled. They came in. As they went in, under the light I saw white hands, wavy hair, white faces, grimacing, gesturing, talking. With them was Brett. She looked very lovely and she was very much with them.
>
> (p. 20)

This early passage carries particular narrative weight in that it marks the first entrance of Brett into the action of the novel and is itself marked, a few sentences later, by a loaded repetition: "And with them was Brett." Yet it is not Brett who elicits Jake's obvious and immediate reaction: "I was very angry. Somehow they always made me angry. I know they are supposed to be amusing, and you should be tolerant, but I wanted to swing on one, any one, anything to shatter that superior, simpering composure" (p. 20). We have here Brett, marked as desirable, set both with and against her companions, who are defined as objects of contempt, derision, and even a smoldering will to violence. But why is Jake so angry? In other words, how do we read his reading of these other men?

To begin with, we can supply the label that Jake (or Hemingway) declines to use. Consistent with the conventions of conversation and censorship of the time, the term "homosexual" remains, so to speak, in the closet. The reader, like Jake, and validating Jake, must read the ostensible sexual preference of the young men from the various signs provided and thereby decode covert private sexuality from overt public sociability. The signs, moreover, must be obvious. Evidence for the unnamed flaw, like the consequences of the unnamed wound, cannot admit alternative interpretations or other possibilities. Still, our reading of Jake and Jake's reading of them are closely conjoined. Metaphorically and literally, both cases set forth sexual and textual absences.[11] Yet a crucial difference, defined precisely as Brett enters the novel, serves to mark one masculine absence as opposed to the other. Jake may be ill-equipped to deal with Brett's sexuality, but not from lack of desire. Lacking such desire, the gay young men who accompany Brett are thus defined as other – not men, not Jake.

The series of signs whereby this negative definition is communicated to the reader is itself highly revealing. We can first infer something of the suspect status of these others from the smile shared by Jake and the attending policeman (policemen, of course, are never wrong in such matters and are never homosexuals themselves). The smile, in short, is itself a code – a secret sign designed to affirm a bond of "true manhood" between Jake and the policeman, and that secret sign is itself underwritten by a more public one, the professional status of the policeman, whose smile carries quite another message than would a similar smile served up under the same circumstances by, say, the women's washroom attendant.

Through such signs as the policeman's smile, these wanting men are sentenced without ever having to be named. Nor are the censoring/censuring signs all external. Consider, for example, the explicitly noted "white hands" and "white faces" of Brett's boys. Since that whiteness does not mark race, what does it token? The suggestion is that the faces are pale, like the powdered faces of women; that the hands are white in contradistinction to the tanned hands of real men – the dark, leathery hands of a Basque shepherd or of the man on the billboard advertising chewing tobacco. Note, too, the "grimacing, gesturing, talking" of this crew (real men are more restrained, reticent) and their willingness to label Georgette, in (strained) contrast to Jake's refusal to label them. "I do declare. There is an actual harlot. I'm going to dance with her" (p. 20), one early observes. And soon, true to Jake's prediction, they all do.

"I knew then that they would all dance with her. They are like that" (p. 20). Jake's retrospectively reported prediction of subsequent behavior both validates his judgment (they were "like that") and smacks of narrative subterfuge (the "like that" is really applied after the fact; it is more a label than a prediction; and it is still more an invitation to label than a label, for the reader must

90

finally decide just what the unspecific "that" entails). Such subterfuge, once it is noted, undermines the very narrative authority that Jake attempts to claim throughout the novel and compromises the judgments made on the basis of that claimed authority. Jake can define the young men on the basis of the distance between them and then have the definition confirm the distance, a process both circular and self-flattering. That same process is also called into question by its own ostensibly unquestionable validity and by the task of judging running, conveniently, only one way.

Matters here are not so simple as Jake might wish. The whole episode, it will be recalled, turns on role confusion, frustration, and deflected sexuality, and does so well before boyish Brett and the girlish young men arrive on the scene. Thus, before we encounter this later odd pairing, we witness Jake and Georgette together. When, in the cab, she broadly hints about what services she is prepared to provide, he "put[s] her hand away" and explains that he is "sick" (p. 15). So when Jake pays for an elaborate dinner for the two of them and discreetly arranges to pay fifty francs for services just as discreetly not rendered, the question of precisely what he is paying for arises. We suggest that it is for the privilege of keeping up appearances, and that keeping up appearances is also what the young men are doing when they arrive with Brett or dance with Georgette. But most of all, the switch in partners suggests, like swinging, the fundamental equivalence of different pairings – Jake and Georgette, Jake and Brett, the young men and Brett, the young men and Georgette. Georgette and Brett (prostitution/promiscuity) are thereby conjoined, and so too are Jake and the boys (sexually maimed/homosexual). In light of these conjunctions, Georgette's labeling, "Everybody's sick. I'm sick too" (p. 16), seems more accurate than Jake's ("They [the homosexuals] are sick") precisely because Georgette does not attempt to postulate any self-flattering distinctions.

We have considered first Jake's interactions with Georgette, Brett, and the young men, and not the opening scene in the book, Jake's expostulations on Robert Cohn, because the narrative self-contradictions in that opening scene have already been assessed elsewhere. As David Wyatt has recently argued, the very excesses of Jake's forced restraint suggest the anger and envy that inform his first words. For Wyatt, Jake's "mistrust [of] all frank and simple people" (p. 4), and particularly of Cohn, rebounds on himself and suggests that "Jake's is the story which doesn't hold together." Jake's "suspicion that perhaps Cohn had never been middleweight boxing champion [of Princeton], and that perhaps a horse had stepped on his face, or that maybe his mother had been frightened or seen something, or that he had, maybe, bumped into something as a young child" (p. 4) arouses the reader's suspicions about Jake. Cohn, Wyatt cogently points out, "emerges as a massive projection of the speaker's anxieties," and "the dominant emotion" in Jake's account "is rage at Cohn's inability to appreciate a potency that he possesses and the narrator lacks." It is not, then, just Cohn whom Jake denigrates but also himself.[12]

The episode with the homosexuals functions in a similar fashion to reveal the contradictions in Jake's own life. His anger, his seemingly absolute dismissal of these men, may well result less from difference than from similarity.[13] Jake relies upon their homosexuality to define his manhood (at least his desire is in the right place), but that definition is tested even as it is formulated by the joint presence of Georgette and Brett. With either woman Jake does not perform, and must gloss over that fact with strained and painful explanation. Furthermore, if encounters with women who expect sexual attention regularly conduce to failure and frustration, no wonder that Jake, for most of the novel, prefers the company of men and finds a day on the river with Bill more satisfying than a night on the town with Brett.[14] But where does that leave Jake, the unmanned manly "man without women"? The terrifying ambiguity of his own sexual limitations and gender preferences may well be one source of his anger (it usually is) with Brett's companions, and another reason why he articulates his anger and hatred for them before he reveals his love for her.

4

When they saw that I had afición, and there was no password, no set questions that could bring it out, rather it was a sort of oral spiritual examination with the questions always a little on the defensive and never apparent, there was this same embarrassed putting the hand on

the shoulder, or a "Buen hombre." But nearly always there was the
actual touching. It seemed as though they wanted to touch you to
make it certain.   (p. 132)

As in the first fragment where Jake and the policeman exchange
a silent sign of their shared sexual identity, the men here again
secretly, silently, jointly proclaim just who and what they are. But
this passage effectively reverses the other in that now it is Jake
who lacks authority, who must be judged. Moreover, like Jake
with the homosexuals, the aficionados assess, without possibility
of appeal, all men (women cannot even be included in the system
of exclusion) who express an interest in bullfighting. Theirs is the
perfect closed system: One either is in or one is not, it takes one to
know one, and if you have to ask how you clearly do not belong.
The very arbitrariness of the unspecified signs affirms their absolute significance. They can, indeed, outweigh other more obvious
signs. The aficionados, for example, even touch in a kind of love,
but with no hint of homosexuality.

Jake seems particularly proud of his membership in what might
well be termed "Club Afición." Inclusion in such select groupings
typically confers status and guarantees "character" even in the
absence of any substantial corroborating evidence such as the large
balance in one's bank account or the glowing testimony of one's
associates – even in the presence of substantial evidence perhaps
pointing in quite another and negative direction. Thus "Montoya
could forgive anything of a bull-fighter who had aficion. He could
forgive attacks of nerves, panic, bad unexplainable actions, all
sorts of lapses. For one who had aficion he could forgive anything.
At once he forgave me all my friends" (p. 132). Jake's other
friends, nonaficionados all, offend against the code. But that of-
fense is also eminently forgivable, and not just because of Jake's
afición.

Those excluded others, like Brett's homosexuals, are required to
define the code. For "everyone an aficionado" signifies the same
as "no one an aficionado," which is to say that the existence of the
club asserts the very differences that its existence requires. It is, of
course, restricted (no Jews need apply); it is male (despite Brett's

93

proclaimed intuitive understanding of bullfighting, she can never belong). It is, as noted, at one and the same time arbitrary and absolute. One cannot buy one's way in, one cannot even earn admission, and yet the grounds of selection are not to be questioned. It is rather like Puritan election vaguely secularized (the "oral spiritual examination") and transposed to twentieth-century Spain. It is of particular importance to the men who belong. Their love of the bullfight confers masculinity by association. Moreover, the masculinity conferred back to the aficionados is itself first conferred by them on the bullfighter. Pedro Romero, when Jake first meets him, "was the best-looking boy [he had] ever seen" (p. 163). One main function of the aficionados is to define this boy as a man, as an icon of manhood, as a bullfighter.

But there is finally something suspect in the aficionados vesting so much of their own manhood in a boylike matador who, through girlish flirtation and enticement, woos a bull to its death.[15] Restrained as their promotion is, these gentle men do protest too much, and the chief proof of that protest is their sustained but covert enterprise of interpretation whereby one sign must be translated into another. Thus the bullfighter's victory becomes the aficionados' victory; his triumph in the ring attests to theirs out of it despite the fact that Romero himself does not fare particularly well outside the ring, as indicated by his fight with Cohn (another defeat turned into victory) or his failed affair with Brett. For the aficionados, however, an artificial bestowing of death tokens a natural mastery over life, and, finally and fundamentally, the phallic trappings of the whole ceremony demonstrate the power and presence of the essential figurative and literal phallus that all "real men" share.

The countering Freudian implications of that last translation are, of course, obvious. An unacknowledged and unacknowledgeable fear of castration is typically masked by overt claims of penile power, which themselves call the proclaimer's manhood further into question even as they assert it. Moreover, not just one premise but the whole program of *afición* turns on duplicitous translation and the repression of undesired "other" readings. Thus the crucial and ostensibly unquestionable assertion of the aficionados as a mystical male brotherhood masks the much more modest claims

of belonging to that brotherhood advanced by particular characters. And again, Jake is paradigmatic. Being an aficionado not only
excuses him for his friends, it excuses him for himself. This second
excuse must not be voiced or examined, yet its covert presence in
the text suggests that the privileged aficionado is also what we well
might term a "de-ficionado" in disguise. Indeed, the whole ethos
of *afición* resembles a sublimation of sexual desire, and the aficionados — serving, guiding, surrounding the matador out of the
ring and applauding him in it — seem all, in a sense, steers.[16]

5

> Romero had the old thing, the holding of his purity of line through
> the maximum of exposure, while he dominated the bull by making
> him realize he was unattainable.   (p. 168)

> Romero smiled. The bull wanted it again, and Romero's cape filled
> again, this time on the other side. Each time he let the bull pass so
> close that the man and the bull and the cape that filled and pivoted
> ahead of the bull were all one sharply etched mass. It was all so slow
> and so controlled. It was as though he were rocking the bull to sleep.
>   (p. 217)

> For just an instant he and the bull were one. (p. 218)

> He became one with the bull. (p. 220)

Immediately before Jake introduces Brett to Pedro Romero,
Mike Campbell, her betrothed, shouts out in drunken insolence,
"bulls have no balls" (p. 175), a phrase he twice repeats as Brett
and Romero exchange their first faltering words, their long, long-
ing glances. Campbell's code is easy to crack. His words only lightly disguise what he fears. As the preceding passages suggest, bulls,
above all, in the symbol system of *afición* are defined by their
difference from steers. Mike's body taunt readily translates, "bulls
are balls, cojones." And so, as Mike also realizes full well, are
bullfighters: "Tell him Brett is dying to know how he can get into
those pants" (p. 176), Mike shouts again, meaning, of course, that
she is dying to know how she can. The covert sexuality in opposition to the imperatives of bullfighting soon becomes more obvious.

Montoya subsequently sees Romero, "a big glass of cognac in his hand, sitting laughing between [Jake] and a woman with bare shoulders, at a table full of drunks. He did not even nod" (p. 177).

Once more the sexual imagery encoded in the text resonates in odd and contradictory ways with other images established in the book. Bulls and bullfighters are defined by their sexuality only when they abstain, only when they flirt with the opposite of sexuality, death. For example, immediately after Romero kills his last bull (the bull with which he was "one"), the boys run "from all parts of the arena" and "dance around the bull" (p. 220) – just as the homosexual men in the first passage discussed danced around Georgette, just as the Spanish men danced around Brett. The dead bull stands in for a living woman in this August fiesta in Pamplona, which itself reenacts an ancient fertility drama. But this is a peculiar drama in which males take all the parts – seducer/seduced, actor/observer, animal/human, male/female. The bullfighter's conquest over the ultimately compliant and submissive bull is, consequently, totally self-referential: the male as signifier and signified, the male as object and subject of his own desire.

Within the context of the ritual, that desire is not for fulfillment but for death. The final erotic embrace of man and beast is an embrace of annihilation. Not only have male and female been elided in this ritual, but sex (life) and death are also hopelessly intermingled. So replete are the sexual innuendoes in the passages describing Romero's conquest of his dark alter ego within the bullring that we are tempted to ask the question (perhaps in a different spirit than Hemingway intended): "Did the earth move for you, too, Pedro?"

The bullfight, it should be emphasized, is not at all simply a fair fight to the finish between man and beast. It is a ritual ceremony enacted by a matador who has trained for years to encounter bulls who have been bred and raised to charge the cape he holds. Only bulls. A "cowfight" does not have the same heroic connotations at all. Moreover, cows, according to bullfight lore, soon pass up the cape to get the man, and so do the wrong kind of bulls. The right bulls make the appropriate substitutions. Just as the matador substitutes bullfighting for sexuality, the bull must elevate "matador fighting" above any other animal promptings (an interest in cows, an affinity for consorting with the steers) and then substitute the cape for the man. Those substitutions support the drama of male domination and man's (not woman's) defeat of nature and death enacted in the ring. It is a drama only shakily supported in that sex and birth seem better ways to the same end, and thus the rigorous exclusion of women. When Jake introduces Brett to Romero, he breaks the club's rules. It is like sex right before the big game, like bringing a woman into the locker room at half time.

It is more than that too. The whole idea of corruption through contact with the female is sustained only by itself – and by the cheerleading aficionados who serve to affirm its validity. The circularity is unmistakable and is also fundamentally at odds with the point and purpose of human sexuality for which the bullfight substitutes. The code of the bullfight can therefore valorize only itself. It cannot serve as a symbol for a more inclusive "meaning" of the novel.

Pedro Romero exists not as a person for the aficionados but as an icon of essential masculinity. When Jake introduces Brett to Romero, he commits the ultimate iconoclasm by transforming Romero from transcendent symbol into a particular person and the subject, furthermore, of Brett's concrete and manifest sexual desire. Jake confuses the symbol with the substance, the icon with the man, and thus offends against not only the code of bullfighting but the whole concept of a code itself. He permits a literalization of spirituality, a degradation of an inviolable code to a set of odd and not particularly significant beliefs. By reducing the code hero, Romero, to a mere individual, a man with human sexual appetites, Jake irrevocably cancels his membership in the club and challenges the very code by which the club and the bullfight exist.

That challenge brings us finally to a question hidden by the text but on which the text turns. As Joanna Russ aptly observes of another Hemingway work: "One cannot stop to ask . . . why killing a large animal will restore Macomber's manhood – everybody knows it will." And since what "everybody knows" is not at issue, "*therefore* the fine details of the story can be polished to that point of high gloss where everything – weather, gestures, laconic conversation, terrain, equipment, clothing – is all of meaning."[17] Hemingway's characteristic laconic style thus assessed is simply the obverse of pervasive cultural codes overdetermined by a surplus of male myths. What can be left out is what is already there. Moreover, what can be left out best demonstrates what is already there; the omnipotence of the work's underlying mythos so "goes without saying" that any "saying" would weaken its case.

Yet an absence proves a presence only if that absence is *read in the right way*. Absence, of course is indeterminate. The text can flirt with other possible readings and even with the negation of its central truths − that is a large part of the text's charm − precisely because it is all along ostensibly safely wed to those truths. Flirtation, however, calls marriage into question. The rebellious reader is tempted to ask the unaskable, especially when that reader sees how much the text itself formulates the unaskable by playing around it and sliding over it. More specifically, when the novel centers on the killing ground of the bullring and the paramount significance of all that transpires there, one can be led to wonder why the death of an animal is supposedly so much more meaningful than the death of a man. Or is it?

6

> Later in the day we learned that the man who was killed was named Vincente Girones, and came from near Tafalla. The next day in the paper we read that he was twenty-eight years old, and had a farm, a wife, and two children. He had continued to come to the fiesta each year after he was married. The next day his wife came in from Tafalla to be with the body. . . . The coffin was loaded into the baggage-car of the train, and the widow and the two children rode, sitting, all three together, in an open third-class railway-carriage. The train started with a jerk, and then ran smoothly, going down grade around the edge of the plateau and out into the fields of grain that blew in the wind on the plain on the way to Tafalla.
>
> (p. 198)

As Linda W. Wagner has observed, the death of Vicente Girones comes precisely at the point where the reader anticipates a different story, either the romantic report of the first passionate exchange between Brett and Pedro Romero or an aficionado's portrayal of the matador courting death in the ring.[18] What we have instead is Girones's death – the only human death reported in the novel's record of different engagements between brave bulls and braver men (the bulls' bravery is forced in that they have no choice in the matter). But this triumph of beast over man occurs as the antithesis of heroic combat – a crowd of men running before the bulls, the bulls "galloping together, heavy, muddy-sided, horns swinging, [until] one shot ahead, caught a man in the running crowd in the back and lifted him in the air" to leave him, gored, dead, "face down in the trampled mud" (pp. 196–7).

The anonymous man, the sudden senseless violent death, the mud – these signs suggest that Vicente Girones's demise is significant in its utter meaninglessness. That suggestion also carries over to the surrounding episodes, to Cohn's previous assault on Jake followed by his attack on Romero, to the subsequent bloody events in the bullring. Cohn has just spurned the role of the spurned lover to fight for Brett "like a man," so presently Romero, although badly bruised, must still confront the "bull who killed Vicente Girones" (p. 199). The first privileged male violence might seem a little dubious, yet is it not redeemed by the second, which is itself magnified by the first? Romero's victory is all the greater because of his injury. But between these two interconnected actions falls the shadow of Girones's death, and that shadow effectively darkens the whole myth of chivalry and the excess of romanticism at the base of both episodes. More to the point, the death of Girones deflates all the rituals of violence. "All for fun. Just for fun" (p. 197), as the waiter testifies. Cohn thrashes Romero; the bull kills Girones; Romero kills the bull; and Brett simply forgets the bull's ear – the trophy, the final empty sign of all this valor – when she leaves town with Romero, an act (his, not hers) that, according to the same code that earlier signified his status as hero, now signifies he is not a true bullfighter. So much for the code. So much for the code hero.

Admittedly, the crowd mourns Girones's death – but not enough to postpone the bullfight. Far from it; the hint of blood merely enhances the excitement still to come. Yet who is this killer, this bull? What does he/it represent? The waiter voices a perturbing answer. Not an aficionado, the waiter asks, "What are bulls?'', and then responds, "Animals. Brute animals" (p. 197). Only by purposely investing the bulls with a special meaning, a ritual significance, can aficionados and matadors convince themselves — the waiter might say "delude" — that something heroic actually takes place in the ring. In other words, the ritual of the fight is a carefully controlled performance in which all participants — aficionados, bullfighter, and bull — collectively enact a fiction of man's triumph over real animal danger and symbolic human death.

The fate and fact of Vicente Girones, however, brings symbolic death into fatal conjunction with the real thing. "You hear?" the waiter says to Jake. "Muerto. Dead. He's dead. With a horn through him. All for morning fun" (p. 198). The repetition of the word "dead," translated from one language to another to emphasize its finality in both, undercuts the ritual at the heart of the code, at the heart of the novel. A man dies so that a bull's ear can be cut off and given to a woman who leaves it in a bed table drawer along with some cigarette butts. What we have here is a devastating critique of the code. Even though the aficionados forget the lesson — Jake too, Jake most of all — in the excitement of the bullfight, the novel still insists that the other side and the underside of the ritual slaughter of the animal is pointless, quotidian human death and that the ritual cannot outweigh or cancel out this other death.

It is finally the widow and children who are left to pay the price for Girones's play at bravery. For notice how we are specifically told that he "continued to come to the fiesta each year after he was married" — as if marriage would normally mean the end of his attendance, his *afición*. But his *afición*, his passion in its bullfight form, becomes literally the end of his marriage. Girones's embracing of the ritual running of the men and the bulls (a plebeian prolegomenon to the bullfight itself) is basically bigamous. You can embrace a wife, children, a simple life on the farm; you can also embrace the life of the fiesta, a thrust of the bull's horn. Vicente Girones made his choice and died to be celebrated by "all the members of the dancing and drinking societies of Pamplona, Estella, Tafalla, and Sanguesa" (p. 198) — to be mourned by the widow and two children, who were barred from the celebration but not from either the funeral or the sad life beyond. "All for sport. All for pleasure" (p. 197).

7

> "He really wanted to marry me. So I couldn't go away from him, he said. He wanted to make it sure I could never go away from him. After I'd gotten more womanly, of course."
>
> (p. 242)

But what is the real significance of the aborted affair, of the possession (and certainty) denied Romero, of the long tresses Brett still refuses to wear? For Richard Hovey and Robert W. Stallman, Romero is finally no better than Cohn. Like Cohn, he both romanticizes and reduces Brett, first by thinking that long hair will make her "more womanly" and second by believing that marriage must put an end to her promiscuous ways.[19] In contrast, Earl Rovit, reading the same passage, sees Brett as no better than Cohn — a romantic who needs to believe that her brief affair with a bullfighter really meant something ("I feel altogether changed" [p. 207], she insists) and that her sending him away was an act of redeeming dignity or even downright heroism: "It's sort of what we have instead of God" (p. 245).[20] Or Mark Spilka finds in this same passage proof positive that Pedro Romero is the book's code hero, that what he wanted was right, and that Brett's refusal to meet her lover's demand demonstrates her fear of womanhood and provides Jake convincing grounds for his final disillusionment with and rejection of her.[21] Clearly, if there is a crucial code underlying the ultimate disposition of the characters, it can be read in different ways.

Rather than attempt to resolve these contradictory readings, we instead observe that they are all implicit within the text and within the reader. Like other seemingly key passages, this one finally admits mostly different entrances into the text. For example, in tone it seems almost a conclusion, and yet it nevertheless still taunts the reader with the very impossibility of at last conclusively accounting for the characters, the book, or the author. Brett admits

101

that "it was rather a knock his being ashamed of me" (p. 242), a new experience for her, obviously, not to be the object of un-qualified male adoration. Does she send Romero away to avoid his judgment of her or to avoid having to accommodate herself to his rigorous (or unreasonable) standards? To avoid corrupting him or to save herself or to preserve safely in memory at least one glorious relationship? Hemingway does not resolve such questions; instead he equates them to similar parallel considerations such as the problematics of Romero's heroism or Jake's. For Brett too has been an icon for most of the novel, the unquestioned/unques-tionable object of Jake's unfulfillable love, the motive for his aban-donment of *afición,* of the code. Was it worth it? Does love conquer all and make everything all right, settle all doubts, resolve all ambiguities? Obviously not. Brett as icon is no more stable than Romero or Jake, and the code of self-fulfilling romantic love is every bit as undercut in the novel as the code of heroic solitary selfhood. And neither can the two codes inhabit the same novel. Thus Brett's most triumphant moment by virtue of one code "I'm thirty-four, you know. I'm not going to be one of these bitches that ruins children" (p. 243) is also, not coincidentally, her greatest defeat by virtue of the other. The code for a woman, although only tangentially considered in this very masculine novel, is, it seems, as arbitrary, inconsistent, and contradictory as the code for a man.

8

"Oh, Jake," Brett said, "we could have had such a damned good time together."
Ahead was a mounted policeman in khaki directing traffic. He raised his baton. The car slowed suddenly pressing Brett against me.
"Yes," I said. "Isn't it pretty to think so?"
THE END   (p. 247)

Critics have tended to read the last line of the novel as Jake's redeeming realization of just where he stands and as a concluding promise, premised on that present awareness, of muted happiness in the future for this enduring and finally honest maimed man. Rovit, for example, argues that his last line demonstrates how "Jake has learned – in part from Count Mippipopolous – that illusions (sure beliefs projected into the future) are the first things one must discard if one wants to learn how to live."[22] Leon Seltzer explicitly subscribes Jake's happiness to come not just to his belated and admittedly covert acknowledgment of his condition but to the underlying impotence itself: "For impotence can actually promote the scrupulously measured detachment that is itself the key to happiness – a happiness that can survive solely through the 'distanced involvement' with reality."[23] But Jake's last words, with the suspended "THE END," do not simply point to a different future beyond the text. Taken in context, they necessarily return us to the text itself and the possibility of having it all to do all over again. Once more a woman presses against him in the cab. The symbolic policeman is again present, and he isn't smiling this time.

That same final dichotomy can be argued in a different way. The promise implicit in Jake's final words is a matter of codes and tone. If Jake claims the awareness that the critics mostly allow him, he can do so only if his question is read as the right statement, a brave declaration of independence and not a pathetic complicity in pretense. That right reading, in turn, depends on the final elevation of the heroic code – or at least the machismo one. If it (heroism or machismo) is at last self-evidently valid and unassailably authentic, then Jake, maimed as he is and ambiguous as his final gesture of manhood might be, must still be read in the right way. A man has to do what a man has to do. But nothing in the novel gives governing status to that ostensibly governing code. Since exercises in heroism are all along entangled with countering exercises in self-defeat, since success requires failure and is in complicity with it, since manliness is defined in terms of womanliness and is inescapably tied to it across the not-dividing slash, why should things be any different at the end?

Far from establishing any concluding finality or promising a different future beyond the text, Jake's last words readily devolve into an endless series of counterstatements that continue the same discourse: "Isn't it pretty to think so"/"Isn't it pretty to think isn't it pretty to think so?" and on ad infinitum, with each term in the sequence an affirmation and a question, a proclamation and a pose, and with each term thrown into a different perspective by the next one in the series. Instead of some redeeming recognition on which Jake can take his last stand, we have, then, implicit in his closing words, / endlessly repeated, and that repetition must finally cancel even itself out, dissolving / to nothingness, to the blank that follows the conclusion of any text. Or put differently, the negation at the end of the novel returns us finally to the promise of its title. As much as the sun rises, the sun also sets, and only the earth – not heroes, not their successes or their failures – abideth forever.

Hemingway apparently thought so too. Writing to Maxwell Perkins in 1926, the author posited his own reading of his text:

> The point of the book to me was that the earth abideth forever. . . . I didn't mean the book to be a hollow or bitter satire but a damn tragedy with the earth abiding forever as the hero.[24]

The observation was offered half as a response to the prevailing criticism of the novel as a "jazz superficial story" about decadent, self-indulgent "brats" or as a satire implicitly condemning those same brats.[25] *The Sun Also Rises* as hedonistic self-glorification; *The Sun Also Rises* as social satire; *The Sun Also Rises* as tragedy: Three different novels were in place as soon as the novel was published. But perhaps the larger point is not that each of these novels (and others) is somehow at odds with all of the others and will the real *The Sun Also Rises* please stand up. We argue instead that it is precisely the self-contradictions in and of the text that make this book still eminently readable even though the Paris of the twenties, pre-Franco Spain, the pride of expatriotism, and the glory of one particular bullfighter are all long gone. Moreover, tragedy, self-gratification, and self-satire are contradictory only if we insist that the self must always be of a piece, must always be free of contradiction, and that fiction, mimetically, must reduce itself to the same univocal understanding. Such reductionism is the ultimate violation of *mimesis* in that life, as humans live it, is rarely so consistent as such critical formulae suggest. The perfectly sustained ambiguity of the novel's final line – "Isn't it pretty to think so?" – should remind the reader that *anagnorisis*, the realization or enlightenment that Aristotle so valued as the redeeming end of the tragic plot, is perhaps no longer possible – if it ever really was – except as a critical coda, a critical ideal, a critical fiction.

Any final meaning of *The Sun Also Rises* hinges, as we have noted, on something as undefined as the vocal inflection of the written word. Depending on how we read Jake's concluding sentence, we can have a sadder and wiser man *or* a man still hoping against hope that, in another time, another place, happiness might yet be possible. But the final sentence is less Jake's sentence – his fate – that the reader's, and the final point is that, returning to the novel's title and the epigraph from Ecclesiastes, the sun *also* rises, the sun *also* sets, and in many of life's lesser and greater moments it's pretty to think, "Isn't it pretty to think so?", saved and condemned by the ambiguities, the merciful incompleteness of the codes that render life both tolerable and terrifying.

NOTES

1. Hemingway deleted this sentence from an early section of the book. Quoted in Michael S. Reynolds, "False Dawn: A Preliminary Analysis of *The Sun Also Rises Manuscript*," in *Hemingway: A Revaluation*, ed. Donald B. Noble (Troy, N.Y.: Whitston, 1983), p. 129.

2. Barbara Johnson, "The Critical Difference: Balzac's 'Sarrasine' and Barthes's 'S/Z,'" in *Untying the Text: A Post-Structuralist Reader*, ed. Robert Young (Boston: Routledge & Kegan Paul, 1981), pp. 165–6. The essay originally appeared in *Diacritics* 8 (June 1978):2–9.

3. Earl Rovit, in *Ernest Hemingway* (New York: Twayne, 1963), noted, for example, that "there is a surprising lack of unanimity among critics on what would seem to be basic non-controversial issues. Critics have divided handsomely on determining where the moral center of the book rests. . . . There have been attempts to read the book as an elegy on the death of love, and others to show that the sun does rise out of the wasteland" (p. 147). Writing a full twenty years later, Andrew Hook begins his essay, "Art and Life in *The Sun Also Rises*," by observing, "Hemingway remains a problem. Has any other modern writer so divided critical opinion?" See *Ernest Hemingway: New Critical Essays*, ed. A. Robert Lee (Totowa, N.J.: Vision and Barnes and Noble, 1983), p. 49.

4. Roland Barthes, *S/Z,* trans. Richard Miller (New York: Hill & Wang, 1974), pp. 3–7.

5. Johnson, "Critical Difference," p. 167.

6. One of the clearest examples of a "code" reading of Hemingway's fiction, style, and life is Ihab Hassan, "Hemingway: Valor against the Void," *The Dismemberment of Orpheus* (New York: Oxford University Press, 1971), pp. 80–109.

7. Frustrated by the reductionist tendency in much Hemingway criticism, Michael S. Reynolds, in *Hemingway's Reading, 1910–40: An Inventory* (Princeton, N.J.: Princeton University Press, 1981), has suggested: "Let us declare a moratorium on nostalgia: on the Hemingway–Callaghan fight, the Dôme cafe, Duff Twysden, on all that public parade" (p. 28).

8. Barthes, *S/Z,* pp. 215–16.

9. Quoted by Barthes, *S/Z,* p. 238.

10. Johnson, "Critical Difference," p. 172–3.

11. Angered over the simpleminded symbol making of critics (and especially the idea that Jake was a "steer because of both his wound and his personality), Hemingway, many years later, provided detailed anatomical descriptions of the wound to emphasize that Jake's problem was not castration but amputation. See his 1951 letter on the subject in Carlos Baker, ed., *Ernest Hemingway: Selected Letters 1917–61* (New York: Scribners, 1981), p. 745, and his comments in an interview with George Plimpton, "The Art of Fiction, XXI: Ernest Hemingway," *Paris Review* 5 (Spring 1958):83.

12. David Wyatt, *Prodigal Sons: A Study of Authorship and Authority* (Baltimore: Johns Hopkins University Press, 1980), p. 57.

13. Nina Schwartz, in "Lovers' Discourse in *The Sun Also Rises:* A Cock and Bull Story," *Criticism* 26 (1984), also perceptively analyzes this passage but applies a Lacanian interpretation to conclude that Jake is actually jealous of the homosexuals because they pose a "threat" to "Jake's privileged relation to Brett. The homosexual is the only other male figure who might be able, like Jake, to evoke in Brett a desire that he would refuse to fulfill" (pp. 58–9).

14. Richard B. Hovey, in *Hemingway: The Inward Terrain* (Seattle: University of Washington Press, 1960), pp. 70–2, notes, for example, that although Jake condemns Cohn's romanticism, Jake is every bit as romantic about the meaningfulness of male bonding, as in the maudlin conversations between Jake, Bill, and the Englishman Harris, who, at the end of their fishing trip, toasts "what this all means to me."

15. Schwartz, "Lovers' Discourse," p. 63–5, convincingly assesses the deflected sexuality and the artificiality of the bullfight and points out how the ritual flirtation with a domesticated animal becomes a substitute seduction.

16. The principal proponent of the "Jake as steer" reading is Philip Young in *Ernest Hemingway: A Reconsideration* (New York: Harcourt Brace, 1966).

17. Joanna Russ, "What Can a Heroine Do? Or Why Women Can't Write?" in *Images of Women in Fiction: Feminist Perspectives,* ed. Susan Koppelman Cornillon (Bowling Green, Ohio: Bowling Green University Popular Press, 1972), p. 12.

18. Linda Welshimer Wagner, *Hemingway and Faulkner: inventors/masters* (Metuchen, N.J.: Scarecrow Press, 1975), p. 44.

19. Hovey, *Hemingway,* p. 65; Robert W. Stallman, *"The Sun Also Rises –* But No Bells Ring," in *The House that James Built* (East Lansing: Michigan State University Press, 1961), pp. 173–93.

20. Rovit, *Hemingway,* p. 156.

21. Mark Spilka, "The Death of Love in *The Sun Also Rises,"* in *Hemingway and His Critics,* ed. Carlos Baker (New York: Hill & Wang, 1961),p. 91.

22. Rovit, *Hemingway,* p. 156.

23. Leon F. Seltzer, "The Opportunity of Impotence: Count Mippipopolous in *The Sun Also Rises,"* *Renascence* 31 (1978):13.

24. Quoted in Baker, *Selected Letters,* p. 229.

25. A selection of early reviews is quoted in Hood, "Art and Life," pp. 52–3.

6

Afterthoughts on the Twenties and *The Sun Also Rises*

JOHN W. ALDRIDGE

1

THE publication in 1973 of Malcolm Cowley's *A Second Flower-ing* reopened once again a question most of us might have preferred to leave closed and may have assumed was long closed. Yet even today it continues to preoccupy us like the puzzle of some ancient unsolved crime, and the occasion of this essay may make it appropriate to explore some of its implications still further.

Just how important, really was the generation of writers who are commonly assumed to have produced a renascence of American literature in the twenties? What is the meaning and value of their contribution from the perspective of all that we know about them and all that has happened in our literature since their time?

Mr. Cowley, having spent more than fifty years studying these writers, may be forgiven if, at seventy-five, he was unable or un-willing to offer much more than a reiteration of opinions that over the years have grown habitual with him and have come to repre-sent the official establishment answer to these questions. His un-derstandably strong feelings of proprietorship toward the twenties writers have caused him to take it for granted that, in spite of individual shortcomings of which he is well aware, they were, on the whole, the most distinguished literary generation the century has so far produced – the most distinguished, in fact, since the great first flowering of American literary talent in the generation of Emerson and Thoreau. Mr. Cowley has written eloquently in sup-port of his position, and one can scarcely fault him for taking it. He

Part 1 of this essay first appeared in different form in *Commentary* (November 1973).

has had a long career as a highly influential critical spokesman for these writers, most of whom were his personal friends. He was on the scene in Paris during the time when they were doing some of their best work, and he was one of the first critics to understand and in *Exile's Return* to explore the significance of the whole artistic phenomenon that so profoundly affected the character of our literature after World War I. In 1973 he said he was conscious of being a last survivor of the twenties generation – left, as he put it, "with the sense of having plodded with others to the tip of a long sandspit where they stand exposed, surrounded by water, waiting for the tide to come in." If anyone has earned the right to his biases, Mr. Cowley surely has.

For the rest of us, the problem of coming to terms with the twenties writers is considerably more complex. We have existed for years in a state of gross informational surfeit, in which we have become so drugged and bored with knowledge concerning every aspect of their lives and works that the possibility of making new and original assessment of them must strike us as being very remote indeed. Furthermore, their achievement as artists is now effectively inseparable in our minds from the legendry of their lives, and their works are so commonly seen as source books of gossip and invitations to nostalgia that no balanced view of their literary merits can be maintained for long.

Many of us also have to contend with our own emotional relation to these writers, a relation that cannot be as intimate and avuncular as Mr. Cowley's but that is no less affected by sentiment or what, in the case of literary people younger than he, has so often been the most abject kind of filial admiration. After all, the twenties generation was once our very special and personal property. We came to love those writers long before it became official wisdom to do so, and there are complex loyalties that bind us equally to them and to that part of ourselves that was formed by their influence. For many of us who discovered them at the right (or perhaps exactly the wrong) age, they seemed quite simply the only *real* writers there were, and so they became our proxy writers. They had all the experiences we would have liked to have, and they wrote exactly the books we wished we might have written. It could be fairly said that they were the first and perhaps the only generation of writers to capture our imagination and to dramatize an image of the literary life with which we could identify because it combined creative achievement with the freedom to explore the fullest possibilities of feeling and being. We may have had the greatest respect for the work of such older men as Dreiser, Mencken, Anderson, and Lewis, but we did not envy them their lives. Their generation seemed gray, remote, and eternally middle-aged. There was something about them that smelled of beer, cigars, pool halls, and the heavy sweat of craft and naturalism. One imagined them going off to the office every morning – pot-bellied businessmen of letters – carrying their inspiration in a lunch pail. But the twenties writers were a very different breed – elegant, aesthetic, temperamentally gifted rather than soberly skilled, as extravagant and wasteful as young British lords, yet profoundly self-preserving in their function as writers. They were distinguished from their elders, above all, by their dedication to the Flaubertian ideal of the artist, their sense of belonging to an aristocratic fraternity of talent. But they also believed in the interdependence of art and experience, the necessity that literature partake of, even as it transformed to suit its own purposes, the felt realities and passions of the individual life.

They thus embodied for us an adolescent ideal that is deeply rooted in the American mythos but that, in recent years, only Norman Mailer has been able to emulate with any conviction, the ideal of the writer as poet-profligate, our fantasy inheritance from the English and French romantics and the disciples of Walter Pater that for the first time among the twenties writers became a practical model of conduct for Americans. Hence, they found it possible to live the life of sensation with great vigor and still live the life of literature with great dedication and success. They were able to have it both ways so splendidly, and they made such excellent use of the opportunity, that some of us will probably never manage to see them except with the high coloration of jealousy or adoration.

Another factor obscuring our view of these writers is that they were largely responsible for developing in us the standards by which we might have been able to judge them. For it was on the evidence of their work and that of their European contemporaries that we formed our first impressions of what literary effects were possible for the modern sensibility. No other standards derived from other historical periods seemed quite applicable to them, if only because so much of their significance resulted from their collective belief that they had transcended the past by confronting a new reality in ways wholly unique to it and to them. Also, in a very real sense, the twenties writers provided the basic assumptions by which we came to perceive, and some of us to express, the experience of the modern world. Their works for a very long time seemed to have done all our essential imagining for us, just as they themselves seemed to have done our essential living, so that we had very little sense of being engaged with life that was not in some way connected with the profoundly seductive images of life with which they first came to dominate our imaginations.

As a result, our view of the literary life of the twenties is a complex mixture of myth and reality, of reality fantasized into myth and myth personalized to the point where it seems like something we ourselves experienced. One does not know, for example, whether the literature created the fantasy or the fantasy found its embodiment in the literary life. But surely a strong attraction of the period for young people was and may still be the fact that it represents their vision of the perfect college literary apprenticeship exported to Paris and prolonged for a decade. The intense, free life of Montparnasse was the idealized equivalent of the intense, free life of the campus literati. There in Paris, happily far away from parents and hometown, it was possible to get drunk as often as one pleased, to stay up all night making love, wander the streets howling into the dawn, be eternally young, sensitive, and promising, do all kinds of experimental work and publish it in the little magazines, be read by an audience of friends who were the perfect classmates, all people of brilliant talent and wit and yet, except for a few, remarkably kind and helpful about one's own work. There too one could enjoy the presence of older teachers and mentors like Pound, Anderson, and Stein, the quintessential writing instructors who were the first to recognize one's gifts and who gave so generously of their advice and encouragement. But perhaps even more important were certain other perquisites of these literary junior years abroad: the advantages of not having to hold down a job because checks were coming regularly from home or one was on a fellowship, not having to be compromised by the bourgeois values of one's parents, not having to worry about marriage and a family, not having responsibilities of any kind except to Art, Truth, and one's friends.

It is not surprising that this image of the Paris literary life should have been embellished in our minds by a cast of personages, both fictional and actual, who have the clarity of outline, the individuality, and the emotional openness that, as a rule, only young people of college age seem to possess. Their appearance and behavior remain with us almost as if recollected from life or recorded in a class yearbook in which we seem to find versions of our own former selves. Nobody will ever be like them again, and nobody will need to be. For these people exist eternally in the roles fixed for them by memory and sentiment – larger than life because they belong to a generation that managed to mythologize its experience while still engaged in the act of having it.

There is the young Jay Gatsby, helplessly in love with the rich and sophisticated sorority girl, holding out his arms to the green light at the end of her boat dock; Amory Blaine proclaiming his valedictory "I know myself but that is all"; Jake Barnes muttering through those bitter, bitter teeth the best line in the senior play, "Yes, isn't it pretty to think so?"; Scott and Zelda, the most popular and beautiful couple on campus, behaving insufferably at parties, jumping fully clothed into the Plaza fountain; Hemingway, the most talented boy in the class, writing his first stories at a table in the Closerie des Lilas; good old Thomas Wolfe, a boy who never seemed to stop growing, getting very drunk, waving his arms, and knocking out the electrical system of an entire town. And we remember the others, the people like Harry Crosby, Slater Brown, William Bird, Robert McAlmon, and the Gerald Murphys, who matter only because they were friends of the famous and now belong to history simply because everyone connected, however remotely, with the Paris literary life in the twenties now belongs to history.

The writers whom Leslie Fiedler once called "great stereotype-mongers" have bequeathed us themselves and their characters as clichés, and criticism has made more clichés out of the essential arguments that can brought against them. Yet the most familiar

113

argument is also the least avoidable. They were a group of highly talented but narrow writers, and their narrowness was most dramatically revealed in the fact that they had one abiding interest – themselves when young, an interest that, in the case of some of them, became the literary preoccupation of a lifetime. Their books had all the attributes of young consciousness. They were lyrical, nostalgic, sentimental, stylish, experimental, and iconoclastic, and they told over and over again the story of self-discovery through the first conquest of experience. We learned from them what it is like to grow up in the small towns of America, how it feels to fall in love, have sex, get drunk, go to war, be an American in Europe, all for the first time, to be so hungry for life that you want to consume all the food, liquor, and women in the world or to discover that the system created by adults is capitalistic and corrupt or hypocritical and dull.

Fitzgerald wrote the story of young romance and riotous youth and, remarkably enough, became famous at twenty-four largely on the strength of the fact that he informed the older generation about just how badly the young really behaved. Hemingway's first and best materials were an adolescent's adventures in Europe, his initiation into the mystery cult of foreign sports, bullfighting, and big-game hunting, the loss of his innocence through the death of his ideals and his love in European war. Dos Passos found his most dependable subject in the totalitarianism of social hierarchies, whether political, economic, or military, in which the integrity of the young was destroyed or severely compromised and the artistic spirit was broken under the grinding pressures of the machine. There are very few people over forty in this literature, and when they do appear, we can usually recognize them by their stigmata of physical ugliness, venality, and hypocrisy. Only the young are truly human. But then the young are doomed to be the victims of the old, to die in their wars, to be tricked by their deceits, ruined through seduction by their false gods.

It is logical that the qualities we remember most clearly in this literature are those that impressed us when we ourselves were young – the marvelous intensity about people and raw experience, the preoccupation with the self, with love, sex, freedom, time, adventure, the irreverence toward the world of the fathers, the disdain for the adult religion of work, self-sacrifice, expediency, competition, and conformity. It is also logical that so many of these writers were able to function effectively only so long as they could keep alive their youthful responses. A number did not live into middle age. Some died romantically young; others, like Fitzgerald, died old while still chronologically young. Of those who survived beyond fifty, almost all were engaged in reiterating the experiences of their youth or continued, as did Hemingway, to write out of a fading memory of emotional and intellectual premises established during the time of their first intense engagement of life.

They were, in fact, the first American literary generation to make being young into both a style of life and a state of grace. It is largely because of their influence that so many Americans are unable to perceive experience except as something that happens to one up to the age of thirty, or to understand that life can on occasion be something other than a process of losing the intensities one was once able to feel. At the end of that fateful confrontation between Gatsby and Tom Buchanan in the Plaza Hotel, Nick Carraway suddenly remembers that it is his thirtieth birthday: "Thirty – the promise of a decade of loneliness, a thinning list of single men to know, a thinning brief-case of enthusiasm, thinning hair." Read for the first time at the age of eighteen, the passage seems one of the most poignant in the novel. But then, perhaps years later, we may come to recognize that our sympathies should go not to Nick but to Fitzgerald. It is *his* limited vision of the possibilities of life that is exposed here, even as it is this same limitation that makes Gatsby a convincing and pathetic character.

One reason, of course, for this preoccupation with youth is that World War I had the effect of seeming to annihilate past history and the old styles of history. Hence, the generation that had fought in the war felt urgently the need to establish new premises, to redefine the terms of existence. Not only was this necessarily a task for youth, but it placed unique and dramatic emphasis on the responses of youth. Only the young were sensitive and adjustable enough to be able to determine whether a given emotion or experience conformed to the new standards of authenticity produced, at least in large part, by the war. Besides, they were the ones who had "been there," been initiated, had heard all the big words and learned that those words did not describe how they felt or what they had been through. Thus, the literature of the twenties is not merely a narcissistic but – as the example of Hemingway makes particularly clear – a testing literature, one in which the effort again and again is to create an accurate new idiom and at the same time to determine the truth or falsity of a radically new, essentially foreign experience – most often according to the responses of a provisional and existential, inevitably youthful self.

Fortunately, there were elements that worked powerfully to the advantage of these writers. First, there was the fact that their consciousness of being unique and their experience unprecedented was validated by social and moral changes so profound that a literary career might be constructed around the process simply of recording them. These writers were in a position to be among the first to witness such changes, and they were aided greatly by what Frederick J. Hoffman once called their creatively "useful innocence," their small-town sensitivity to forms of conduct that, in spite of their surface sophistication, they could not help judging by the provincial standards they had been brought up on. It is not surprising that some of their best work has the incandescent quality of the astonished spectator, privileged to be on the scene of first encounters involving people who suddenly seem no longer to know by what assumptions they should behave.

Second, their prolonged apprenticeship in Europe enabled them to view American life from the perspective not only of distance but of adversary cultural values. They had inherited from their predecessors – most notably Lewis, Mencken, and Van Wyck Brooks – an intellectual arrogance, a disdain for bourgeois society, and a belief in the absolute supremacy of art and the artist that were formed into a metaphysics under the tutelage of Stein and Pound. They became cosmopolitan provincials abroad; they learned to judge America by essentially elitist European standards; and of course, they found America provincial. But since they were themselves provincial, their attitudes retained a dimension of ambivalence that helped to humanize their satire and finally made it seem an expression more of regret than of contempt.

They had, in short, a strong sense of belonging to or being able to identify imaginatively with place, perhaps just because they

116

were physically so displaced – not only from home but from the past represented by home. They may have been creatively stimulated by the experience of living in a dramatic, radically changing present. But they could also feel anxious and uncertain and in need of the structures of coherence and identity they had left behind in the Midwest and South. This undoubtedly accounts for the fact that Hemingway and Fitzgerald were so continuously preoccupied with procedural questions, with the effort to formulate dependable rules of feeling and conduct. Hemingway's works can be read as a series of instruction manuals on how to respond to and behave in the testing situations of life now that the rules have changed and the world has become, in effect, an unknown foreign country. It might also be argued that some of his most dependable instructions are those he was able to reclaim from the past, in particular the American frontier past, the lessons of courage, fidelity, honor, and rectitude that might still have the power to influence human conduct when all other values were being called into question. Fitzgerald's best novels are restatements of Henry James's great theme: the implications of the misuse of power over those who are innocent and helpless by those who are strong and unscrupulous.

In short, one finds in these writers and in some of their contemporaries a concern with the moral authenticity of certain traditions they might have presumed to be outmoded. It may be expressed only in a nostalgic return to the locales that provided security in childhood – Hemingway's Big Two-Hearted River or Wolfe's Old Catawba. But it may also involve complex loyalties and codes of honor that once gave a human dimension to life – as Nick Carraway discovers through the experience of Gatsby and Dick Diver through his marriage to Nicole. Both men derived a ''sense of the fundamental decencies'' from their fathers, and so can evaluate and ultimately condemn a society in which such decencies no longer have meaning.

One of the very best of Fitzgerald's stories, ''Babylon Revisited,'' is yet another expression of the desire to reconstitute certain values of moral discipline and self-control after the violent dissipations of the decade that ended in bankruptcy in 1929. Charlie Wales, a battered survivor of the time, returns to Paris in the hope of regaining custody of his daughter. To do this, he must prove to his sister-in-law that he has become a fit and responsible person. He very nearly succeeds in convincing her, but fails at the last moment when two of his old drinking friends reappear and destroy his chances of making a new life. Just as Nick after Gatsby's death wanted "the world to be in uniform and at a sort of moral attention forever," so Charlie felt the need "to jump back a whole generation and trust in character again as the eternally valuable element." But there is no escape from the consequences of his wasted past: "Again the memory of those days swept over him like a nightmare – the people they had met traveling; the people who couldn't add a row of figures or speak a coherent sentence . . . the women and girls carried screaming with drink or drugs out of public places . . . The men who locked their wives out in the snow, because the snow of twenty-nine wasn't real snow. If you didn't want it to be snow, you just paid some money."

The act of moral reclamation may be a necessity for every literary generation. In America we do not so much build on tradition as steal from it those elements we think may help us to understand the always unprecedented experience of our own time. The twenties writers had a singular relation to the problem. They had the strongest sense that their experience was indeed unprecedented and that the older modes of literary statement were inadequate to describe it. They therefore became excessively preoccupied with their own experience and, in both their writing and their lives, with the innovative and the defiant. For reasons of temperament and historical position, many became fixated permanently at the level of *rite de passage,* where they were condemned forever to play the roles of rebellious sons and wayward daughters, able to find their identity only in the degree of their opposition to the literary and social conventions of the past.

Yet, in reviewing their achievement, one is struck by how often their most admirable qualities seem to have been revealed at those rare moments when the writer was able, perhaps by accident, perhaps out of desperation, to transcend the limits of the adversary stance and define his materials in some clear relation to the sustaining values of an older moral tradition or a newly created artistic convention based on those values. If Fitzgerald and Hemingway experienced such moments, as some of their best work, most notably *The Great Gatsby* and *The Sun Also Rises,* would seem to indicate, they did so only occasionally, in part because the life of their own time absorbed them too completely, and they were so rarely able to see that life from a consistently maintained moral perspective.

All that Dos Passos essentially had to support his intricately panoramic vision of American society were the values of an adversary politics, and it is significant that as he grew older, his vision did not deepen; only his politics aged. E. E. Cummings and Hart Crane were, in their very different ways, poetically adversary. Cummings made a limited kind of artistic convention out of wit and irreverence, whereas Crane, like Wolfe, sought all his life for a convention that would give shape and significance to the chaotic responses of his personality. Both poets had the defect of being confined by personality, and Crane in particular existed in that state of psychic nihilism in which, as Allen Tate once observed, "any move is possible because none is necessary."

The examples of Faulkner and, on a less exalted level, Thornton Wilder should serve to remind us that there were alternatives to the more fashionable positions taken by so many of the twenties generation. There were alternatives *if* one possessed, as Wilder did, an intellectual culture broad enough to enable one to draw creatively on the best resources of the Western literary tradition or *if* one had Faulkner's access to the abundant resources of the Southern tradition. But without these advantages, supplemented by talent of very large size, too many of the twenties writers remained locked into their first youthful responses to an experience that was too overwhelmingly intense to serve as very much more than the material of an often brilliant but very personal and limited literature. They may be forever established in our minds as the immensely charismatic personages of one of the most dramatic decades in our literary history. But it is significant that we can never separate them from the image we retain of the life of their time, just as they were unable, except at rare moments, to separate themselves and, in so doing, to become larger than their experience, its imaginative possessors and masters, the shapers of those truths it contained that might have made timeless in art what is otherwise lost to history.

2

Today, twenty-five years after his death, it can fairly be said that of the several gifted writers of that remarkable generation, Hemingway is the one who still makes the strongest claim on our attention. Critical and biographical studies of Faulkner, Fitzgerald, Dos Passos, and some of the others continue to be produced. But one senses in their case that the fundamental interpretations have been made, the perimeters of essential discussion established, and that very little of much surprise or value remains to be discovered about them.

In the case of Hemingway, on the other hand, discussion not only goes forward but seems since his death to have accelerated massively, with no indication of an end in view. Along with a seven-story mountain of critical literature, we now have on public display the biased testimony of just about everybody who ever knew him, was related or married to him, or slept, fished, hunted, or went to war with him. We have the recollections of his literary contemporaries, the opinions of those former friends who sat for their portraits in *The Sun Also Rises*, the memoirs of his siblings, his sons, and his favorite Paris bartenders. We have his letters and his manuscripts and all those photographs – Bwana Hemingway stalking kudu on the plains of Africa, commanding his native gun bearers in terse Swahili; War Correspondent Hemingway in perilous service with the Spanish loyalists; Submarine-chaser Hemingway at the wheel of the *Pilar*, patrolling the waters around Cuba for Nazis; Task Force Hemingway in big Papa beard and swathed in ammunition belts, leading his ragtag band of irregulars on intrepid sorties behind the enemy lines. And of course, the image of him that emerges is protean. Evidently, he was a vital, rude, crude, sensitive, kind, unkind, generous, selfish, jealous, petty, helpful, hurtful, loving, and hating human being who did not care terribly much for anything or anyone except the things that excited and diverted him and the people who amused him, adored him, or encouraged and supported him in his work. The more we know about him, the less we like him, yet the more we find him fascinating. There was never before in our literary history a writer of such force of personality, such public presence, so highly skilled in the complex art of self-manufacture and self-promotion that he created and embodied our very conception of literary celebrity in this age.

Since 1961, the sheer volume of critical and biographical information about Hemingway has reached the proportions of a corporate industry, with branches and subsidiaries spreading across the world into virtually every civilized country where his work has been translated and published. The immediate result has been to inflate still further the already overblown Hemingway legend and to elevate almost everything he wrote, both the best and the worst, to the status of holy scripture, while he himself is securely established as the imperial icon of American literature in the first half of the twentieth century.

The information glut, along with the deification process, has had a curiously ambiguous effect: it has informed us so thoroughly about the life and character of the man that we feel compelled to reexamine the work for evidence of the virtues that would perhaps justify the attention and honor accorded the writer. Yet it has also made it impossible for us to recapture that virginity of mind with which we first read him and were able to appreciate, without the inflammation of awe and reverence, the many excellent features of his artistry. For now we are confronting not a writer but an international literary monument, and the works that once seemed real and alive have become – as Mary McCarthy so admirably said about Salinger's Glass family writings – "the sacred droppings of holy birds." There is much irony in the fact that Gertrude Stein foresaw it all while meaning something else altogether when she observed that Hemingway "looks like a modern and . . . smells of the museums." And it is in the museum showcases of the world's adoration, among the Egyptian mummies, the ancient relics and artifacts, that Hemingway's works are now forever on public view.

To extricate them from the museums and restore them to life is an impossible task. But with a sufficiently vigorous exercise of imagination, it may be possible to approach them once again and ask some of the first questions, the kind that, in our virginity of mind, we were once able to answer and that all the subsequent celebrity has almost caused us to forget how to ask.

What was it then, and what is it now, that makes Hemingway so compellingly attractive as a writer? What is the nature and source of the very great pleasure we take in him when he is at his best and the pain we feel when he is at his worst? To begin with the obvious, and accepting the pretense that we are reading him for the first time, let us say that Hemingway's initially most seductive attribute was and remains his powerful responsiveness to experience. It is an attribute perhaps made more seductive by the fact that most of us since his time have found it to be seriously diminished in ourselves. One reason is that our responses to the infinitely more complex and diffuse experiences of our present world have *had* to diminish if we are to retain our sanity. Another reason is that so few of us today have, or have ever had, access to a clearly defined microcosmic world in which the things one feels, says, and does might take on the sacramental importance they had for Hemingway in World War I, in Paris, and later in Spain. It is as if we had all suffered some brain damage as the price we have had to pay for existence in the second half of the twentieth century, a loss of acute responsiveness to the life around us, even as our sense that the vitality of that life has itself declined forces us into a troubled and abstracted self-preoccupation.

One does not easily envy the life of any of our immediate contemporaries – the talent, perhaps, but not the life – as one so easily envies Hemingway's, particularly during the years when his talent was freshest and he was writing at the top of his form in those early stories and *The Sun Also Rises,* his first and, withal, still his best novel. He was young then, as we were young when we first read him. He was living, as we regrettably were not, in the most exotic city in Europe among some of the most remarkable personalities and gifted artists of the post–World War I era. And he brought to it all the highly sensitized perspective of the provincial midwestern tourist viewing with wonder and delight the hitherto undiscovered riches of foreignness.

He took the greatest pleasure – and gave us, vicariously, the greatest pleasure – in the hotels, bars, and restaurants of Paris, and with his quickly acquired inside-dopester knowingness, he appointed himself the official instructor in where and how to live wisely and well. He could recite the names of all the streets; he knew the exact location of all the good places and the best route to take to get to them; and he was on friendly terms with the best bartenders and waiters who worked in them. He had a wonderful eye not only for quality but for terrain, whether the topography of Paris or the landscape of Spain, and in sharing his knowledge with us, he schooled us in the ways of a world we did not know but desperately wished we did.

He also accomplished something far more significant for us and for literature. If he had not, then Scott Fitzgerald's well-known description of *The Sun Also Rises* as "a romance and a guidebook" might have been all that needed to be said. But in introducing us literally to the life of foreignness, Hemingway at the same time created the illusion that *every* element of life is in fact foreign, hence new and without precedent in the known experience of the past. Every element needs, therefore, to be carefully examined and tested to determine the degree of its authenticity. In order to live an authentic life and produce an authentic fiction, one has to proceed with the greatest caution and select only those experiences, express only those emotions, that have proved their validity because they have been measured against the realities of honest feeling and what one senses in one's deepest instincts to be true. The result in Hemingway's fiction is not a realistic reflection of a world but the literal manufacture of a world, piece by piece, out of the most meticulously chosen and crafted materials.

It is a world that is altogether strange and perilous because it is without moral history and received standards of conduct. Characters, therefore, most move through it as if through enemy-territory, learning how to live while trying to stay alive. To survive they need all the cunning and expertise they can muster. They must be sure that they know at all times exactly where they are, both geographically and in relation to others. They must also learn exactly how to behave so as to minimize the risk of becoming vulnerable to error and the dangerous consequences of losing self-control. They must fabricate, through constant study and trial, an etiquette that will enable them to know instinctively what is appropriate and what is not, so that they can maintain decorum under stress or siege. They must master the procedure for everything, the correct methods for carrying out their function – whether it is hunting, fishing, bullfighting, or eating and drinking. And above all, they must know the cost of everything, not only the cost in money but the physical and emotional cost. To survive successfully is to learn how to get one's money's worth, the right return on the investment; hence, one must be extremely careful to make only the *right* investments, those that will yield honest satisfactions and beneficial emotions rather than lead to the overinflation of specious values and destructive emotions.

The characters in *The Sun Also Rises* might all be seen to be morally measurable on the basis of whether or not they are wise enough to get their money's worth. Jake Barnes is one who is constantly preoccupied with cost. He tells us what meals cost in restaurants, how much it is proper to tip waiters and bellmen in order to be assured of a satisfactory return in attentive service, who borrowed how much from whom and whether the debt was promptly repaid (Mike Campbell borrows constantly from everybody and never repays). In Bayonne after the disastrous end of the fiesta, Jake is pleased to be back in France because there "everything is on such clear financial basis. . . . If you want people to like you you have only to spend a little money" (243). Earlier in Pamplona, while indulging in some drunken philosophizing, he concludes that "you paid some way for everything that was any good. I paid my way into enough things that I liked, so that I had a good time. Either you paid by learning about them, or by experience, or by taking chances, or by money. Enjoying living was learning to get your money's worth and knowing when you had it" (153).

Count Mippipopolous has learned to get his money's worth and knows when he has. Robert Cohn does not know because he never understands the rate of exchange. His values have not been submitted to the test of actual experience and cannot be, for they have come out of books and romantic fantasy. He is therefore unable to see Brett for what she is, although exactly what she is never becomes altogether clear. Because of the count's wisdom about money as well as his arrow wounds, Brett identifies him as "one of us," which he may or may not be, since he has already learned what she and Jake are still trying to learn, namely, how to live decorously and well. Brett fails from the beginning because Jake's wound prevents her from fulfilling what she believes to be her true love for him. In compensation, she has affairs and she plans to marry Mike, about whom she does not appear to care very much, presumably because he will one day be rich. She has had an interlude with Cohn in San Sebastian, mostly because she was bored at the time, and she comes to despise Cohn because he is so obviously not "one of us" and refuses to believe that the affair did not mean anything.

Such values as Brett has are in limbo through the greater part of the novel and become operative only momentarily and feebly when she decides to send Romero away. There is finally no hope for her because she has been undisciplined and adrift for too long. She has never learned the value of anything, has given up or never taken control of her life, and so has passed into the control of random impulse and boredom. In the ultimate sense of the word, Brett is lost. That is the poignant message behind Jake's closing remark about the prettiness of thinking that things might ever have been different between them. Nor will things ever be different between her and Mike. He may inherit a fortune, but one can be sure that neither of them will get his money's worth because neither knows how to.

Hemingway's tight minimalist style, which is displayed in its purest form in *The Sun Also Rises,* is the precise verbal expression of the view of life that dominates and finally evaluates the action of the novel. If Hemingway believed, as he clearly did, that if the right, carefully selected experiences are chosen and only the proper emotions expressed, the result will be an absolutely authentic fictional world containing nothing that will ever ring false, then the language, chosen with equal care, so authentically simple and basic, is the perfect fastidious statement of the morally fastidious world it is designed to create. The vacant spaces between and behind the words, the strongly sensed presence of things omitted, become expressive of all the alternatives and elaborations, all the excesses and equivocations of language, that have been scrupulously rejected in the style's formation. The emphasis given to the individual words and phrases that seem so much larger than they are just because they have escaped rejection makes it appear that a verbal artifact is being constructed or salvaged, word by word, from a junk heap of redundancy and imprecision. There are no moral or literary precedents to provide the style with foundation or scaffolding. Everything that manages, against great resistance, to achieve utterance is seemingly being uttered for the very first time in human history, is a kind of Ur-statement of primordial truth. It is a method whose ultimate effect is incantatory and catechistic, and what is being prayed to and propitiated is the demon god of flux and excess, that force of anarchy that drives most of the characters toward ruin and that it is the task of the language to redeem and convert into a force of artistic order.

Such a method, composed as it is of a minimum of simple words that seem to have been squeezed onto the page against a great compulsion to be silent, creates the impression that those words – if only because there are so few of them – are sacramental, and the frequent reappearance of some of them in the same or similar order at intervals throughout the text tends to give them idiographic value. Thus, "nice" and the phrase "one of us" become the pervasive but hollow designations of moral judgment in the novel, and the hollowness is perfectly consonant with the theme. In a similar way, some of the characters become idiographs when a certain distinctive feature of their appearance or behavior is established in our minds as their identifying logo or psychological autograph – again because Hemingway describes them so sparingly that what little he does say about them takes on something of the quality of a Homeric epithet. Thus, Jake is personified by his impotence, Bill Gorton by his passion for stuffed animals, Brett by her mannish hats and hairstyle, the Count by his arrow wounds, Robert Cohn by his romanticism. In each case, furthermore, the defining detail becomes revelatory of the character's dramatic role and thematic meaning, so that what begins as a novel of manners ends as a moral allegory about people who lack the moral substance even to follow the code of behavior that they profess to honor. Jake is unmanned and Brett is defeminized. Bill Gorton's passion is for things that look like the real thing but are actually dead. The Count has been wounded by arrows, which must make him as anachronistic as his fancy title and tastes supported by income from a chain of sweet-shops must make him ludicrous.

Brett with her title is also an anachronism, as is Mike, the stereotypical wastrel aristocrat with his stereotypical prospects of one day inheriting a fortune. And Cohn's romanticism, which is the central irritant in the novel, is yet another. All represent former sources of value that no longer have value. Cohn's sentimentalized vision of love belongs to that part of the nineteenth century that was supposedly killed in World War I, and its resurrection in the aftermath can only mean trouble for people who are also resurrected casualties, stuffed human animals, to whom any feeling, when aggressively acted upon, is a threat to psychic harmony and the security of nonfeeling.

In his study of American modernism, *A Homemade World*, Hugh Kenner makes the extremely perceptive observation that "Hemingway's achievement . . . consisted in setting down, so sparely that we can see past them, the words for the action that concealed the real action." There is abundant evidence for this everywhere in *The Sun Also Rises*. Jake's strength as a character derives in large part from his capacity for withholding information. We are constantly aware in the novel of the presence of what we are not told, of what Jake refuses to acknowledge and judge because it is too dangerous to make a judgment and thus bring the danger to the surface of consciousness. As Carl Jung wrote in *Psychology and Religion*, "consciousness must have been a very precarious thing in its beginning. . . . Even an ordinary emotion can cause a considerable loss of consciousness. Primitives therefore cherish elaborate forms of politeness, speaking with a hushed voice, laying down their weapons, crouching. . . . Before people of great authority we bow with uncovered head, i.e., we offer our head unprotected in order to propitiate the powerful one, who might easily fall suddenly a prey to a fit of uncontrollable violence." And Otto Fenichel says in *Psychoanalytical Theory of Neurosis* that "trauma creates fear of every kind of tension . . . because even a little influx of excitement may have the effect of 'flooding' the patient" or, in Jung's terms, causing him to lose consciousness and go berserk.

For the elaborately polite because clearly traumatized characters of this novel, consciousness is so precarious and fragile that any kind of tension is to be feared and, if possible, ignored. One can safely respond to only the barest minimum of sensory stimuli – the look of the landscape, the physical pattern of an action, especially when strictly ritualized, what people monosyllabically said to one another. But there must be little or nothing revealed about how anyone really felt, what deeper emotions were aroused by the various conflicts and confrontations. It is part of the magic of the minimalist style that we know almost nothing – and we scarcely miss knowing – about Jake's emotional state throughout the major part of the novel, nor do we know much of anything about the nature of the relationship between Brett and Mike and between Jake and Bill. This information is carefully withheld or we are led to believe that it is revealed in actions that occur in the background or offstage. But the omissions make a statement that there is some acute unpleasantness here that cannot be directly confronted because it is a threat to psychic equilibrium and might cause a dangerous "flooding" of consciousness.

It has often been said that the dramatic movement of *The Sun Also Rises* is through a series of alternating scenes of conflict and recuperation from conflict. The fishing interlude in Burguete and Jake's holiday in San Sebastian both represent rest and curative periods following the stressful experiences, first of Paris, then of Pamplona. In both, emotional decorum is almost fanatically maintained. Nothing is allowed to occur that might impose a strain or precipitate a crisis, and this is made easier to accomplish, significantly enough, by the fact that in Burguete there are only men without women and in San Sebastian only one man alone in the good company of himself.

In both, attention is kept focused on matters of physical procedure: exactly how a fishhook is baited and with what, what kind of box lunch was provided by the hotel, just how cold the wine was, what dinner cost. And we are told just how Jake in San Sebastian went about putting his things away in his room and the movements he made as he went from the hotel to the beach and changed his clothes in a bathing-cabin, put on his bathing suit, and went swimming, then how he came out of the water, lay on the beach until he was dry, then went into the bathing-cabin, took

128

off his suit, sloshed himself with fresh water, and rubbed dry. It is all as meticulously choreographed as the fishing routine in "The Big Two-Hearted River" and for the same reason — because the real situation cannot be confronted, the real story cannot be told.

Gertrude Stein, in one of her famous pronouncements on Hemingway, said that there is in fact a real story to be told about Hemingway, one that he should write himself, "not those he writes but the confessions of the real Hemingway." Clearly, Hemingway did not write it and could not because the real story was too deeply disturbing to tell, just as the young Nick Adams could not bring himself to enter the shadowy part of the river where it ran into the swamp — because "in the swamp fishing was a tragic adventure." But the remarkable fact is that in telling as much or as little of the story as he did, Hemingway managed through his complex artistry to use words in such a way that we are indeed allowed to see past them and to glimpse the outlines of the mysterious and probably tragic adventure that the words were not quite able to describe but were also not quite able to conceal.

If the thing most feared is barely visible behind the language, the fear itself is barely controlled by the language. Language is a provisional barricade erected against the nihilism that threatens to engulf Hemingway's characters, the nihilism that is always seeking to enter and flood the human consciousness. Hemingway at his best offered us a portrait that did not need to be painted of a condition we recognize everywhere around and within us, and he gave us as well our only means of defense against it — the order of artistic and moral form embodied in a language that will not, in spite of everything, give up its hold on the basic sanities, will not give up and let out the shriek of panic, the cry of anguish, that the situation logically calls for. That, and not any of the bravura exploits behind his celebrity, constituted his heroism, and that was the lesson in heroism he had to teach. Of his many qualities, that was the one that most deserved, and continues to deserve, our admiration and loyalty.

Notes on Contributors

John W. Aldridge is Professor of English at the University of Michigan and the author of numerous books on contemporary American literature and culture, including *After the Lost Generation, In Search of Heresy, The Devil in the Fire,* and *The American Novel and the Way We Live Now.* He is also a contributor to *The New York Times Book Review, Harper's, Sewanee Review,* and other publications.

Arnold E. Davidson is Professor of English at Michigan State University. He has written books on Mordecai Richler, Jean Rhys, and Joseph Conrad; has coedited a book on Margaret Atwood; and has published many articles on modern Canadian, British, and American fiction.

Cathy N. Davidson, Professor of English at Michigan State University, currently holds awards from the American Council of Learned Societies and the John Simon Guggenheim Foundation. Her most recent books are *Revolution and the Word: The Rise of the Novel in America,* and editions of America's first best-selling novels, *The Coquette* and *Charlotte Temple* (all from Oxford University Press, 1986). She has also written extensively on Ambrose Bierce, Canadian fiction, women's fiction, and American fiction.

Scott Donaldson, Louise G. T. Cooley Professor of English at the College of William and Mary, is the author of a number of essays and books on American literature. He has written four biographies: *Poet in America: Winfield Townley Scott; By Force of Will: The Life and Art of Ernest Hemingway; Fool for Love, F. Scott Fitzgerald;*

and *John Cheever: A Biography* (due in 1987). He has held senior Fulbright lectureships in Finland and Italy, and taught as Bruern Fellow at the University of Leeds.

Wendy Martin, Professor of English at Queens College and editor of *Women's Studies,* has recently published *An American Triptych: Anne Bradstreet, Emily Dickinson, Adrienne Rich.* She is editing the Colonial section of the anthology *Reconstructing American Literature.*

Michael Reynolds, Professor of English at North Carolina State University, has published three important books on Ernest Hemingway: *Hemingway's First War, Hemingway's Reading 1910–1940,* and *The Young Hemingway,* which was a nonfiction finalist in the American Book Awards for 1986. He is presently completing a literary biography of Hemingway's Paris years.

Linda Wagner-Martin has written extensively on modern American poetry and prose, with books on William Carlos Williams, Denise Levertov, Ernest Hemingway, William Faulkner, John Dos Passos, and Ellen Glasgow, among others. Her biography of Sylvia Plath will be published in 1987. She teaches at Michigan State University, where she is Professor of English and editor of *The Centennial Review.*

Selected Bibliography

A comprehensive bibliography of scholarship on Ernest Hemingway or *The Sun Also Rises* is beyond the scope of this collection. The books listed here are just some of the most important reference works and critical studies for the student to recognize; there are many others. Essayists included in this collection have used the Scribners paperback edition of *The Sun Also Rises*.

Baker, Carlos. *Ernest Hemingway: A Life Story.* New York: Scribners, 1969.
    (ed.) *Hemingway and His Critics: An International Anthology.* New York: Hill & Wang, 1961.
    (ed.) *Ernest Hemingway: Critiques of Four Major Novels.* New York: Scribners, 1962.
    (ed.) *Ernest Hemingway: Selected Letters, 1917–1961.* New York: Scribners, 1981.
Baker, Sheridan. *Ernest Hemingway: An Introduction and Interpretation.* New York: Holt, Rinehart & Winston, 1967.
Benson, Jackson. *Hemingway: The Writer's Art of Self Defense.* Minneapolis: University of Minnesota Press, 1969.
    (ed.) *The Short Stories of Ernest Hemingway: Critical Essays.* Durham, N.C.: Duke University Press, 1975.
Catalog of the Ernest Hemingway Collection at the John F. Kennedy Library. Boston: G. K. Hall, 1982.
Donaldson, Scott. *By Force of Will: The Life and Art of Ernest Hemingway.* New York: Viking, 1977.
Grebstein, Sheldon Norman. *Hemingway's Craft.* Carbondale: Southern Illinois University Press, 1973.
Hanneman, Audre. *Ernest Hemingway: A Comprehensive Bibliography.* Princeton, N.J.: Princeton University Press, 1969 and Supplement, 1975.
Kert, Bernice. *The Hemingway Women.* New York: W. W. Norton, 1983.
Meyers, Jeffrey, ed. *Hemingway, The Critical Heritage.* London: Routledge & Kegan Paul, 1982.

Reynolds, Michael. *Hemingway's First War: The Making of "A Farewell to Arms."* Princeton, N.J.: Princeton University Press, 1976.

"False Dawn: *The Sun Also Rises* Manuscript" in *A Fair Day in the Affections: Literary Essays in Honor of Robert B. White, Jr.*, ed. Jack D. Durant and M. Thomas Hester. Raleigh, N.C.: Winston Press, 1981.

Hemingway's Reading, 1910–1940. Princeton, N.J.: Princeton University Press, 1982.

Rovit, Earl. *Ernest Hemingway.* New York: Twayne, 1963.

Sarason, Bertram D. *Hemingway and the Sun Set.* Washington, D.C.: Microcard Editions, 1972.

Stephens, Robert O., ed. *Ernest Hemingway: The Critical Reception.* New York: Burt Franklin & Co., 1977.

Wagner, Linda W. *Ernest Hemingway: A Reference Guide.* Boston: G. K. Hall, 1977.

(ed.) *Ernest Hemingway: Five Decades of Criticism.* East Lansing: Michigan State University Press, 1974.

Hemingway and Faulkner: inventors/masters. Metuchen, N.J.: Scarecrow Press, 1975.

Waldhorn, Arthur. *A Reader's Guide to Ernest Hemingway.* New York: Farrar, Straus & Giroux, 1972.

Watts, Emily Stipes. *Ernest Hemingway and the Arts.* Urbana: University of Illinois Press, 1971.

Weeks, Robert P., ed. *Hemingway: A Collection of Critical Essays.* Englewood Cliffs, N.J.: Prentice-Hall, 1962.

White, William, ed. *Byline: Ernest Hemingway.* New York: Scribners, 1967.

(ed.) *The Merrill Studies in "The Sun Also Rises."* Columbus, Ohio: Charles E. Merrill Publishers, 1969.

Young, Philip. *Ernest Hemingway: A Reconsideration.* University Park: Pennsylvania State University Press, 1966.